HowExpert Guide to Dating and Relationships

The Ultimate Guide to Finding, Building, and Sustaining Lifelong Love and Connection

HowExpert

Copyright © 2024 Hot Methods, Inc. DBA HowExpert™
www.HowExpert.com

For more tips related to this topic, visit HowExpert.com/dating.

Recommended Resources

- HowExpert.com – How To Guides on All Topics from A to Z by Everyday Experts.
- HowExpert.com/free – Free HowExpert Email Newsletter.
- HowExpert.com/books – HowExpert Books
- HowExpert.com/courses – HowExpert Courses
- HowExpert.com/clothing – HowExpert Clothing
- HowExpert.com/membership – HowExpert Membership Site
- HowExpert.com/affiliates – HowExpert Affiliate Program
- HowExpert.com/jobs – HowExpert Jobs
- HowExpert.com/writers – Write About Your #1 Passion/Knowledge/Expertise & Become a HowExpert Author.
- HowExpert.com/resources – Additional HowExpert Recommended Resources
- YouTube.com/HowExpert – Subscribe to HowExpert YouTube.
- Instagram.com/HowExpert – Follow HowExpert on Instagram.
- Facebook.com/HowExpert – Follow HowExpert on Facebook.
- TikTok.com/@HowExpert – Follow HowExpert on TikTok.

Publisher's Foreword

Dear HowExpert Reader,

HowExpert publishes quick 'how to' guides on all topics from A to Z by everyday experts.

At HowExpert, our mission is to discover, empower, and maximize everyday people's talents to ultimately make a positive impact in the world for all topics from A to Z…one everyday expert at a time!

HowExpert guides are written by everyday people just like you and me, who have a passion, knowledge, and expertise for a specific topic.

We take great pride in selecting everyday experts who have a passion, real-life experience in a topic, and excellent writing skills to teach you about the topic you are also passionate about and eager to learn.

We hope you get a lot of value from our HowExpert guides, and it can make a positive impact on your life in some way. All of our readers, including you, help us continue living our mission of positively impacting the world for all spheres of influences from A to Z.

If you enjoyed one of our HowExpert guides, then please take a moment to send us your feedback from wherever you got this book.

Thank you, and I wish you all the best in all aspects of life.

To your success,

Byungjoon "BJ" Min 민병준
Founder & Publisher of HowExpert
HowExpert.com

PS…If you are also interested in becoming a HowExpert author, then please visit our website at HowExpert.com/writers. Thank you & again, all the best! John 3:16

COPYRIGHT, LEGAL NOTICE AND DISCLAIMER:

COPYRIGHT © 2024 HOT METHODS, INC. (DBA HOWEXPERT™). ALL RIGHTS RESERVED WORLDWIDE. NO PART OF THIS PUBLICATION MAY BE REPRODUCED IN ANY FORM OR BY ANY MEANS, INCLUDING SCANNING, PHOTOCOPYING, OR OTHERWISE WITHOUT PRIOR WRITTEN PERMISSION OF THE COPYRIGHT HOLDER.

DISCLAIMER AND TERMS OF USE: PLEASE NOTE THAT MUCH OF THIS PUBLICATION IS BASED ON PERSONAL EXPERIENCE AND ANECDOTAL EVIDENCE. ALTHOUGH THE AUTHOR AND PUBLISHER HAVE MADE EVERY REASONABLE ATTEMPT TO ACHIEVE COMPLETE ACCURACY OF THE CONTENT IN THIS GUIDE, THEY ASSUME NO RESPONSIBILITY FOR ERRORS OR OMISSIONS. ALSO, YOU SHOULD USE THIS INFORMATION AS YOU SEE FIT, AND AT YOUR OWN RISK. YOUR PARTICULAR SITUATION MAY NOT BE EXACTLY SUITED TO THE EXAMPLES ILLUSTRATED HERE; IN FACT, IT'S LIKELY THAT THEY WON'T BE THE SAME, AND YOU SHOULD ADJUST YOUR USE OF THE INFORMATION AND RECOMMENDATIONS ACCORDINGLY.

THE AUTHOR AND PUBLISHER DO NOT WARRANT THE PERFORMANCE, EFFECTIVENESS OR APPLICABILITY OF ANY SITES LISTED OR LINKED TO IN THIS BOOK. ALL LINKS ARE FOR INFORMATION PURPOSES ONLY AND ARE NOT WARRANTED FOR CONTENT, ACCURACY OR ANY OTHER IMPLIED OR EXPLICIT PURPOSE.

ANY TRADEMARKS, SERVICE MARKS, PRODUCT NAMES OR NAMED FEATURES ARE ASSUMED TO BE THE PROPERTY OF THEIR RESPECTIVE OWNERS, AND ARE USED ONLY FOR REFERENCE. THERE IS NO IMPLIED ENDORSEMENT IF WE USE ONE OF THESE TERMS.

NO PART OF THIS BOOK MAY BE REPRODUCED, STORED IN A RETRIEVAL SYSTEM, OR TRANSMITTED BY ANY OTHER MEANS: ELECTRONIC, MECHANICAL, PHOTOCOPYING, RECORDING, OR OTHERWISE, WITHOUT THE PRIOR WRITTEN PERMISSION OF THE AUTHOR.

ANY VIOLATION BY STEALING THIS BOOK OR DOWNLOADING OR SHARING IT ILLEGALLY WILL BE PROSECUTED BY LAWYERS TO THE FULLEST EXTENT. THIS PUBLICATION IS PROTECTED UNDER THE US COPYRIGHT ACT OF 1976 AND ALL OTHER APPLICABLE INTERNATIONAL, FEDERAL, STATE AND LOCAL LAWS AND ALL RIGHTS ARE RESERVED, INCLUDING RESALE RIGHTS: YOU ARE NOT ALLOWED TO GIVE OR SELL THIS GUIDE TO ANYONE ELSE.

THIS PUBLICATION IS DESIGNED TO PROVIDE ACCURATE AND AUTHORITATIVE INFORMATION WITH REGARD TO THE SUBJECT MATTER COVERED. IT IS SOLD WITH THE UNDERSTANDING THAT THE AUTHORS AND PUBLISHERS ARE NOT ENGAGED IN RENDERING LEGAL, FINANCIAL, OR OTHER PROFESSIONAL ADVICE. LAWS AND PRACTICES OFTEN VARY FROM STATE TO STATE AND IF LEGAL OR OTHER EXPERT ASSISTANCE IS REQUIRED, THE SERVICES OF A PROFESSIONAL SHOULD BE SOUGHT. THE AUTHORS AND PUBLISHER SPECIFICALLY DISCLAIM ANY LIABILITY THAT IS INCURRED FROM THE USE OR APPLICATION OF THE CONTENTS OF THIS BOOK.

HOT METHODS, INC. DBA HOWEXPERT
EMAIL: SUPPORT@HOWEXPERT.COM
WEBSITE: WWW.HOWEXPERT.COM
COPYRIGHT © 2024 HOT METHODS, INC. (DBA HOWEXPERT™)
ALL RIGHTS RESERVED WORLDWIDE.

Table of Contents

Recommended Resources 2
Publisher's Foreword 3
Book Overview 22
Introduction 31
   The Importance of Dating and Relationships 31
      1. Emotional Well-being 31
      2. Personal Growth 31
      3. Social Connection 32
      4. Physical Health 32
      5. Life Satisfaction 32
   How to Use This Guide for Maximum Benefit 33
      1. Read Sequentially 33
      2. Reflect and Apply 33
      3. Stay Open-Minded 33
      4. Engage Actively 34
      5. Revisit and Review 34
   Key Themes in Dating and Relationships 34
      1. Self-Understanding 35
      2. Communication 35
      3. Finding a Partner 35
      4. Building and Sustaining Relationships 35
      5. Advanced Relationship Dynamics 36
      6. Enhancing and Sustaining Relationships 36
      7. Endings and New Beginnings 36
   Conclusion of the Introduction 36
Part 1: Understanding Yourself 38
Chapter 1: Self-Discovery and Personal Growth 38
   1.1 Identifying Your Values and Goals 38
      A. Reflect on Your Beliefs 38
      B. Assess Your Priorities 39
      C. Set Clear Goals 39
      D. Align Your Actions 40
   1.2 Building Self-Esteem and Confidence 41
      A. Practice Self-Acceptance 41
      B. Challenge Negative Thoughts 42
      C. Set Achievable Goals 42
      D. Surround Yourself with Positive Influences 43
      E. Engage in Self-Care 43
   1.3 Overcoming Past Relationship Baggage 44
      A. Acknowledge Your Feelings 44

- B. Learn from Past Experiences 45
- C. Seek Professional Help if Needed 46
- D. Forgive Yourself and Others 46
- E. Create New Narratives 47
- 1.4 Developing a Positive Mindset 47
  - A. Practicing Gratitude 48
  - B. Maintaining Optimism 48
  - C. Engaging in Positive Self-Talk 49
  - D. Surrounding Yourself with Positivity 49
  - E. Visualizing Success 50
  - F. Practicing Mindfulness and Meditation 50
- Chapter 1 Review: Self-Discovery and Personal Growth 51
- Chapter 2: Emotional Intelligence 54
  - 2.1 Understanding Your Emotions 54
    - A. Identify Your Emotions 54
    - B. Analyze Impact 55
    - C. Mindfulness Practice 56
  - 2.2 Empathy and Understanding Others 56
    - A. Active Listening 57
    - B. Ask Open-Ended Questions 57
    - C. Reflect and Paraphrase 58
    - D. Observe Nonverbal Cues 58
    - E. Put Yourself in Their Shoes 59
  - 2.3 Managing Stress and Anxiety 59
    - A. Identify Sources of Stress 60
    - B. Develop a Stress-Relief Routine 60
    - C. Practice Deep Breathing 61
    - D. Time Management 61
    - E. Seek Support 62
  - 2.4 Developing Healthy Coping Mechanisms 63
  - A. Positive Self-Talk 63
  - B. Physical Activity 63
  - C. Creative Outlets 64
  - D. Problem-Solving Skills 65
  - E. Healthy Lifestyle Choices 65
  - F. Relaxation Techniques 66
  - Chapter 2 Review: Emotional Intelligence 67
- Chapter 3: Defining Your Relationship Needs 70
  - 3.1 Identifying Your Relationship Goals 70
    - A. Reflect on Past Relationships 70
    - B. Determine What You Want in a Partner 71

- C. Consider Long-Term vs. Short-Term Goals 72
- D. Align Goals with Personal Values 72
- E. Visualize Your Ideal Relationship... 73
- F. Write Down Your Goals... 74
- 3.2 Understanding Your Love Languages 74
  - A. Words of Affirmation 75
  - B. Acts of Service 75
  - C. Receiving Gifts... 76
  - D. Quality Time 77
  - E. Physical Touch 77
  - F. To Understand Your Love Language: 78
- 3.3 Setting Boundaries and Expectations....................................... 79
  - A. Identify Your Boundaries 79
  - B. Communicate Clearly... 80
  - C. Be Respectful and Considerate 80
  - D. Revisit and Adjust.. 81
  - E. Handle Conflicts Constructively 81
- 3.4 Recognizing Red Flags and Deal Breakers.............................. 82
  - A. Identify Your Non-Negotiables 83
  - B. Be Aware of Common Red Flags 83
  - C. Trust Your Intuition 85
  - D. Seek External Perspectives 85
  - E. Take Action 85
- Chapter 3 Review: Defining Your Relationship Needs 86
- Chapter 4: Basics of Effective Communication................................ 90
  - 4.1 The Foundations of Communication 90
    - A. Clarity and Conciseness... 90
    - B. Honesty and Openness 91
    - C. Respect and Empathy 91
    - D. Feedback and Reflection... 92
    - E. Timing and Context... 93
  - 4.2 Active Listening Techniques 93
    - A. Pay Full Attention 94
    - B. Show Interest... 94
    - C. Reflect and Paraphrase.. 94
    - D. Ask Open-Ended Questions 95
    - E. Avoid Interrupting... 95
    - F. Respond Thoughtfully 95
  - 4.3 Nonverbal Communication Cues.. 96
    - A. Body Language 96
    - B. Facial Expressions... 97

    C. Eye Contact 97
    D. Tone of Voice 98
    E. Personal Space 98
    F. Touch 99
  4.4 Navigating Difficult Conversations 99
    A. Prepare Mentally and Emotionally 100
    B. Choose the Right Time and Place 100
    C. Stay Calm and Composed 101
    D. Use "I" Statements 101
    E. Listen Actively and Empathetically 102
    F. Seek to Understand, Not Win 102
    G. Stay Focused on the Issue 103
    H. Agree on Action Steps 103
  Chapter 4 Review: Basics of Effective Communication 104
Chapter 5: Enhancing Communication in Relationships 107
  5.1 Expressing Yourself Clearly 107
    A. Be Direct and Specific 107
    B. Use "I" Statements 108
    C. Stay on Topic 108
    D. Be Honest and Authentic 109
    E. Check for Understanding 109
    F. Practice Active Listening 110
  5.2 Digital Communication Etiquette 110
    A. Be Mindful of Tone 110
    B. Respond Promptly 111
    C. Use Emojis and Punctuation 112
    D. Avoid Sensitive Topics via Text 112
    E. Respect Privacy 113
    F. Limit Over-Communication 113
  5.3 Conflict Resolution Strategies 114
    A. Stay Calm and Composed 114
    B. Focus on the Issue, Not the Person 115
    C. Listen Actively 115
    D. Seek Common Ground 116
    E. Use Problem-Solving Techniques 116
    F. Take Breaks if Needed 117
    G. Agree to Disagree 117
  5.4 Apologizing and Forgiving 118
    A. Offer a Sincere Apology 118
    B. Explain the Impact 119
    C. Commit to Change 119

- D. Allow Time for Healing 120
- E. Practice Self-Forgiveness 120
- F. Seek Forgiveness Gracefully 121
- G. Discuss Forgiveness Openly 121
- Chapter 5 Review: Enhancing Communication in Relationships 122

Part 3: Finding a Partner 125
Chapter 6: Modern Dating Landscape 125
- 6.1 Online Dating and Apps 125
  - A. Choosing the Right Platform 125
  - B. Creating an Engaging Profile 126
  - C. Safety First 127
  - D. Effective Communication 127
  - E. Managing Expectations 128
  - F. Setting Up Dates 128
- 6.2 Traditional Dating Methods 129
  - A. Social Events and Gatherings 129
  - B. Hobbies and Interests 130
  - C. Networking Events 130
  - D. Introductions Through Friends and Family 131
  - E. Volunteering 131
- 6.3 Navigating Social Media in Dating 132
  - A. Building a Positive Online Presence 132
  - B. Using Social Media for Connection 133
  - C. Balancing Privacy and Transparency 133
  - D. Avoiding Misinterpretations 134
  - E. Managing Relationship Status Online 134
- 6.4 Balancing Dating with Personal Life 135
  - A. Prioritizing Self-Care 135
  - B. Setting Boundaries 136
  - C. Communicating Expectations 136
  - D. Scheduling Quality Time 137
  - E. Reflecting on Your Priorities 137
  - F. Evaluating Relationships 138
- Chapter 6 Review: Modern Dating Landscape 139

Chapter 7: Creating an Attractive Profile 142
- 7.1 Crafting a Compelling Bio 142
  - A. Be Authentic 142
  - B. Showcase Your Personality 143
  - C. Keep It Concise 143
  - D. Include a Call to Action 144
  - E. Be Positive 144

  F. Proofread 145
 7.2 Choosing the Right Photos 145
  A. Use High-Quality Images 145
  B. Show Your Face 146
  C. Include a Variety of Shots 146
  D. Avoid Group Photos 147
  E. Be Authentic 147
  F. Update Regularly 148
 7.3 Communicating Effectively Online 149
  A. Start with a Strong Opening Message 149
  B. Be Respectful and Polite 149
  C. Ask Open-Ended Questions 150
  D. Share About Yourself 150
  E. Use Proper Grammar and Spelling 151
  F. Be Patient 152
 7.4 Safety Tips for Online Dating 152
  A. Protect Your Personal Information 153
  B. Use the Platform's Messaging System 153
  C. Trust Your Instincts 154
  D. Do a Background Check 154
  E. Meet in Public Places 155
  F. Have a Safety Plan 155
  G. Be Cautious with Photos and Social Media 156
 Chapter 7 Review: Creating an Attractive Profile 156
Chapter 8: Meeting People Offline 160
 8.1 Expanding Your Social Circle 160
  A. Join Clubs and Groups 160
  B. Attend Workshops and Seminars 161
  C. Volunteer for Causes You Care About 161
  D. Take Up New Hobbies 162
  E. Socialize at Work 162
 8.2 Attending Social Events and Gatherings 163
  A. Be Open and Approachable 163
  B. Attend a Variety of Events 164
  C. Leverage Your Interests 164
  D. Network Strategically 165
  E. Bring a Friend 166
 8.3 Approaching and Talking to Strangers 166
  A. Overcome Initial Hesitation 167
  B. Use Openers and Icebreakers 167
  C. Practice Active Listening 168

- D. Be Confident and Authentic 168
- E. Respect Boundaries 169
- F. Practice Makes Perfect 169
- 8.4 Utilizing Mutual Connections 170
  - A. Let Your Network Know 170
  - B. Attend Gatherings with Mutual Connections 171
  - C. Ask for Introductions 172
  - D. Follow Up on Introductions 172
  - E. Maintain and Nurture Connections 173
- Chapter 8 Review: Meeting People Offline 173
- Chapter 9: The First Date 177
- 9.1 Planning the Perfect First Date 177
  - A. Choose the Right Venue 177
  - B. Consider Interests and Preferences 178
  - C. Plan for Comfort 178
  - D. Keep It Simple 179
  - E. Have a Backup Plan 179
  - F. Set a Time Limit 180
- 9.2 Making a Great First Impression 180
  - A. Be Punctual 180
  - B. Dress Appropriately 180
  - C. Greet Warmly 181
  - D. Show Genuine Interest 181
  - E. Maintain Positive Body Language 181
  - F. Be Yourself 182
- 9.3 Effective Communication on a Date 182
  - A. Start with Light Conversation 182
  - B. Ask Open-Ended Questions 182
  - C. Share About Yourself 183
  - D. Listen Actively 183
  - E. Avoid Controversial Topics 183
  - F. Be Respectful 183
- 9.4 Evaluating Compatibility 184
  - A. Assess Conversation Flow 184
  - B. Observe Body Language 184
  - C. Consider Shared Interests and Values 185
  - D. Evaluate Emotional Connection 185
  - E. Check Your Comfort Level 185
  - F. Reflect on Red Flags 185
- Chapter 9 Review: The First Date 186
- Part 4: Building a Relationship 189

Chapter 10: Early Stages of a Relationship 189
  10.1 Understanding the Honeymoon Phase 189
    A. Characteristics of the Honeymoon Phase 189
    B. Emotional Intensity...189
    C. Setting Realistic Expectations 190
    D. Enjoy the Moment..190
  10.2 Setting the Foundation for Trust 190
    A. Be Honest and Transparent 191
    B. Keep Promises 191
    C. Communicate Openly 191
    D. Show Respect 191
    E. Be Reliable..192
    F. Address Issues Promptly 192
  10.3 Navigating Differences and Conflicts 192
    A. Acknowledge Differences...192
    B. Stay Calm and Respectful...193
    C. Practice Active Listening..193
    D. Seek Common Ground 193
    E. Compromise and Collaborate 194
    F. Take Breaks if Needed 194
  10.4 Establishing Healthy Communication Patterns 194
    A. Be Clear and Direct 194
    B. Use "I" Statements..195
    C. Practice Active Listening..195
    D. Share Positive Feedback...195
    E. Create a Safe Space...196
    F. Schedule Regular Check-Ins 196
    G. Be Patient and Understanding 196
  Chapter 10 Review: Early Stages of a Relationship................................197
Chapter 11: Developing Trust and Intimacy 200
  11.1 The Importance of Trust in Relationships 200
    A. Foundation for Emotional Safety 200
    B. Enhances Communication 200
    C. Builds Reliability and Dependability...201
    D. Supports Conflict Resolution 201
    E. Promotes Emotional and Physical Intimacy 201
  11.2 Building Trust Over Time 202
    A. Be Honest and Transparent 202
    B. Keep Your Promises 202
    C. Show Respect and Understanding 202
    D. Communicate Openly and Frequently..203

- E. Admit Mistakes and Apologize 203
- F. Be Supportive and Reliable 203
- G. Give Trust to Receive Trust 203
- 11.3 Developing Emotional and Physical Intimacy 204
  - A. Emotional Intimacy 204
  - B. Physical Intimacy 204
- 11.4 Maintaining Boundaries and Respect 205
  - A. Identify Your Boundaries 205
  - B. Communicate Clearly 206
  - C. Respect Boundaries Consistently 206
  - D. Revisit Boundaries Regularly 206
  - E. Handle Boundary Violations Constructively 206
  - F. Balance Togetherness and Independence 207
- Chapter 11 Review: Developing Trust and Intimacy 207

Chapter 12: Deepening Connection 210
- 12.1 Building Emotional Intimacy 210
  - A. Open and Honest Communication 210
  - B. Active Listening 210
  - C. Vulnerability 211
  - D. Emotional Support 211
  - E. Regular Check-Ins 211
  - F. Express Appreciation 211
- 12.2 Exploring Physical Intimacy 212
  - A. Communication About Physical Needs 212
  - B. Affectionate Touch 212
  - C. Creating a Comfortable Environment 212
  - D. Exploring Together 213
  - E. Respecting Boundaries 213
  - F. Maintaining Regular Intimacy 213
- 12.3 Shared Experiences and Activities 214
  - A. Common Interests 214
  - B. Try New Things Together 214
  - C. Daily Rituals 214
- 12.4 Maintaining Individuality within a Relationship 216
- Chapter 12 Review: Deepening Connection 217

Chapter 13: Long-Term Relationship Success 221
- 13.1 Sustaining Love and Affection 221
  - A. Regular Expressions of Love 221
  - B. Physical Affection 221
  - C. Quality Time 222
  - D. Shared Interests 222

  E. Keep the Fun Alive 222
  F. Express Gratitude 222
 13.2 Effective Conflict Resolution 223
  A. Stay Calm and Respectful 223
  B. Listen Actively 223
  C. Focus on the Issue, Not the Person 224
  D. Seek to Understand 224
  E. Take Breaks if Needed 224
  F. Follow Up 224
 13.3 Supporting Each Other's Growth 225
  A. Encourage Individual Goals 225
  B. Celebrate Achievements 225
  C. Provide Emotional Support 225
  D. Share Growth Experiences 226
  E. Respect Independence 226
  F. Be a Source of Inspiration 226
 13.4 Planning for the Future Together 227
  A. Discuss Long-Term Goals 227
  B. Set Joint Goals 227
  C. Create a Financial Plan 227
  D. Plan for Life Changes 228
  E. Build a Support Network 228
  F. Revisit and Adjust Plans 228
 Chapter 13 Review: Long-Term Relationship Success 229
Part 5: Advanced Relationship Dynamics 232
Chapter 14: Navigating Serious Commitments 232
 14.1 Moving In Together 232
  A. Discuss Expectations 232
  B. Create a Financial Plan 232
  C. Choose the Right Space 233
  D. Establish Boundaries 233
  E. Communicate Openly 233
 14.2 Engagement and Marriage 234
  A. Discuss Marriage Goals 234
  B. Plan the Proposal 234
  C. Engagement Period 234
  D. Premarital Counseling 235
  E. Plan the Wedding 235
  F. Focus on the Marriage 235
 14.3 Blending Families and Parenting 235
  A. Open Communication 236

    B. Build Relationships with Stepchildren 236
    C. Set Clear Roles and Boundaries 236
    D. Create New Family Traditions 236
    E. Seek Support 237
    F. Prioritize Couple Time 237
  14.4 Financial Planning and Shared Goals 237
    A. Open Financial Communication 237
    B. Set Financial Goals 238
    C. Create a Budget 238
    D. Emergency Fund 238
    E. Invest Wisely 238
    F. Regular Financial Check-Ins 239
  Chapter 14 Review: Navigating Serious Commitments 239
Chapter 15: Dealing with External Influences 243
  15.1 Managing Relationships with In-Laws 243
    A. Establish Boundaries 243
    B. Show Respect and Appreciation 243
    C. Communicate Openly 244
    D. Spend Quality Time Together 244
    E. Support Your Partner 244
    F. Seek Common Ground 244
  15.2 Balancing Friends and Your Relationship 245
    A. Communicate Your Needs 245
    B. Prioritize Quality Time 245
    C. Include Your Partner 246
    D. Respect Each Other's Friendships 246
    E. Set Boundaries 246
    F. Regular Check-Ins 246
  15.3 Handling Social Media and Privacy 247
    A. Discuss Social Media Boundaries 247
    B. Respect Privacy 247
    C. Monitor Interactions 248
    D. Limit Social Media Use 248
    E. Handle Conflicts Offline 248
    F. Be Transparent 248
  15.4 Coping with Life Changes and Stress 249
    A. Communicate Openly 249
    B. Offer Support and Empathy 249
    C. Develop Coping Strategies 250
    D. Maintain Routine and Stability 250
    E. Focus on Teamwork 250

F. Seek External Support 250
Chapter 15 Review: Dealing with External Influences 251
Chapter 16: Specific Relationship Types 254
16.1 Long-Distance Relationships 254
A. Building Trust and Communication 254
B. Creative Ways to Stay Connected 255
C. Planning Visits and Future Moves 255
D. Overcoming Unique Challenges 256
16.2 Intercultural and Interfaith Relationships 256
A. Navigating Cultural Differences 256
B. Respecting and Understanding Beliefs 257
C. Blending Traditions and Practices 257
D. Communicating with Family and Friends 258
16.3 Relationships with Different Life Circumstances 258
A. Dating After Divorce or Loss 258
B. Dating with Children 259
C. Dating in Different Age Groups (Teenage, 30s, Seniors) 259
D. Managing Health and Wellness in Relationships 260
Chapter 16 Review: Specific Relationship Types 260
Part 6: Enhancing and Sustaining Relationships 263
Chapter 17: Keeping the Spark Alive 263
17.1 Planning Date Nights and Getaways 263
A. Set a Schedule 263
B. Be Creative 263
C. Plan Mini Getaways 264
D. Unplug and Focus 264
E. Plan Together 264
17.2 Exploring New Activities Together 264
A. Try New Hobbies 265
B. Take Classes Together 265
C. Attend Events 265
D. Travel and Explore 265
E. Challenge Each Other 266
17.3 Keeping Romance and Passion Alive 266
A. Express Affection Daily 266
B. Leave Love Notes 266
C. Plan Romantic Surprises 267
D. Compliment and Appreciate 267
E. Create Intimate Moments 267
F. Maintain Physical Intimacy 268
17.4 Surprising Each Other 268

    A. Plan Thoughtful Surprises 268
    B. Celebrate Small Wins 268
    C. Spontaneous Adventures 269
    D. Unexpected Gifts 269
    E. Special Occasions 269
  17.5 Communicating Openly and Honestly 270
    A. Regular Check-Ins 270
    B. Active Listening 270
    C. Express Yourself Clearly 270
    D. Handle Conflicts Constructively 271
    E. Show Empathy and Understanding 271
  17.6 Building and Maintaining Trust 271
    A. Be Reliable and Consistent 272
    B. Honesty is Key 272
    C. Embrace Transparency 272
    D. Practice Forgiveness and Move Forward 272
    E. Support Each Other 273
  17.7 Growing Together 273
    A. Set Shared Goals 273
    B. Encourage Personal Growth 273
    C. Reflect and Adapt 274
    D. Celebrate Growth 274
    E. Stay Curious 274
  Chapter 17 Review: Keeping the Spark Alive 275
Chapter 18: Personal Growth and Relationship Development 279
  18.1 Encouraging Each Other's Dreams 279
    A. Show Genuine Interest 279
    B. Provide Emotional Support 279
    C. Celebrate Small Wins 280
    D. Help Set Goals 280
    E. Offer Practical Help 280
    F. Be Patient and Understanding 280
  18.2 Continuing Education and Learning Together 281
    A. Take Classes Together 281
    B. Read and Discuss Books 281
    C. Attend Seminars and Webinars 281
    D. Explore Online Courses 282
    E. Share Knowledge 282
    F. Set Learning Goals 282
  18.3 Supporting Each Other Through Changes 283
    A. Open Communication 283

  B. Be a Source of Stability 283
  C. Show Empathy 283
  D. Be Flexible 283
  E. Problem-Solve Together 284
  F. Encourage Self-Care 284
 18.4 Celebrating Milestones and Achievements 284
  A. Acknowledge Milestones 285
  B. Plan Special Celebrations 285
  C. Give Thoughtful Gifts 285
  D. Share the Joy 285
  E. Reflect on the Journey 286
  F. Express Gratitude 286
 Chapter 18 Review: Personal Growth and Relationship Development.... 286
Part 7: Endings and New Beginnings 290
Chapter 19: Recognizing When to End a Relationship 290
 19.1 Identifying Unhealthy Patterns 290
  A. Constant Conflict 290
  B. Lack of Trust 290
  C. Emotional or Physical Abuse 291
  D. Controlling Behavior 291
  E. Persistent Unhappiness 291
  F. Isolation 291
  G. Lack of Communication 292
 19.2 Understanding When to Let Go 292
  A. Irreconcilable Differences 292
  B. No Effort to Improve 292
  C. Loss of Respect 293
  D. Personal Growth Stagnation 293
  E. Emotional Detachment 293
  F. Constant Negative Impact 293
 19.3 Planning a Respectful Breakup 294
  A. Choose the Right Time and Place 294
  B. Be Honest but Kind 294
  C. Listen and Acknowledge 294
  D. Avoid Prolonging the Breakup 295
  E. Discuss Practical Matters 295
  F. Offer Closure 295
 19.4 Healing and Moving Forward 295
  A. Allow Yourself to Grieve 296
  B. Seek Support 296
  C. Focus on Self-Care 296

D. Reflect and Learn 296
E. Set New Goals 297
F. Stay Open to New Beginnings 297
Chapter 19 Review: Recognizing When to End a Relationship 297
Chapter 20: Rebuilding After a Breakup 301
20.1 Self-Care and Healing 301
A. Allow Yourself to Feel 301
B. Physical Well-Being 301
C. Mental Health Support 301
D. Engage in Relaxation Techniques 302
E. Create a Self-Care Routine 302
F. Avoid Unhealthy Coping Mechanisms 302
20.2 Learning from Past Relationships 303
A. Reflect on the Relationship 303
B. Identify Patterns 303
C. Recognize Red Flags 303
D. Acknowledge Positive Aspects 304
E. Take Responsibility 304
F. Set New Relationship Goals 304
20.3 Rebuilding Confidence and Trust 305
A. Focus on Self-Improvement 305
B. Positive Self-Talk 305
C. Set Boundaries 305
D. Surround Yourself with Positive Influences 305
E. Gradual Trust-Building 306
F. Forgive Yourself and Others 306
20.4 Opening Yourself to New Possibilities 306
A. Embrace Change 307
B. Expand Your Social Circle 307
C. Stay Open-Minded 307
D. Set Realistic Expectations 307
E. Explore New Interests 308
F. Be Patient 308
Chapter 20 Review: Rebuilding After a Breakup 308
Chapter 21: New Beginnings 311
21.1 Embracing Change and Growth 311
A. Accept the Past 311
B. Adopt a Growth Mindset 311
C. Set New Goals 311
D. Stay Positive 312
E. Seek Inspiration 312

- F. Celebrate Progress ... 312
- 21.2 Rediscovering Yourself ... 313
  - A. Reflect on Your Interests ... 313
  - B. Practice Self-Compassion ... 313
  - C. Prioritize Self-Care ... 313
  - D. Build Self-Confidence ... 313
  - E. Reconnect with Values ... 314
- 21.3 Building a New Vision for the Future ... 314
  - A. Clarify Your Aspirations ... 314
  - B. Develop a Strategic Plan ... 315
  - C. Cultivate a Positive Mindset ... 316
  - D. Stay Flexible and Adaptable ... 316
- 21.4 Finding Love Again ... 317
  - A. Heal Fully First ... 317
  - B. Know What You Want ... 317
  - C. Be Open-Minded ... 318
  - D. Take Things Slow ... 318
  - E. Communicate Clearly ... 318
  - F. Trust Your Instincts ... 318
  - G. Enjoy the Journey ... 319
- Chapter 21 Review: New Beginnings ... 319

Conclusion ... 322
- Reflecting on Your Relationship Journey ... 322
  - 1. Review Milestones and Achievements ... 322
  - 2. Identify Key Learnings ... 322
  - 3. Acknowledge Growth ... 322
  - 4. Appreciate the Journey ... 323
  - 5. Journal Your Thoughts ... 323
  - 6. Discuss with Your Partner ... 323
- Continuing to Grow and Learn ... 324
  - 1. Set Personal and Relationship Goals ... 324
  - 2. Embrace Lifelong Learning ... 324
  - 3. Stay Open to Feedback ... 324
  - 4. Practice Self-Reflection ... 324
  - 5. Cultivate Resilience ... 325
  - 6. Maintain Healthy Relationships ... 325
  - 7. Engage in New Experiences ... 325
- Final Thoughts ... 325
- Final Note ... 326

Appendices ... 327
- Glossary of Dating & Relationship Terms from A to Z ... 327

 Recommended Reading and Resources 330
  Books 330
  Websites and Online Resources... 331
  Podcasts 331
  Worksheets and Exercises 332
  Contact Information for Relationship Support Services 333
 About the Publisher HowExpert... 334
About the Author 335
About the Publisher 336
Recommended Resources 337

Book Overview

If you want to transform your dating life and build meaningful connections, then "HowExpert Guide to Dating and Relationships" is the book for you. This comprehensive guide offers practical advice and actionable steps to navigate the complex world of dating and relationships, from self-discovery to sustaining a long-term partnership.

Introduction

- The Importance of Dating and Relationships: Understand why healthy relationships are crucial for personal fulfillment.

- How to Use This Guide for Maximum Benefit: Learn how to effectively utilize this book to enhance your dating journey.

- Key Themes in Dating and Relationships: Explore the core concepts and principles that will guide you through each stage of dating and relationships.

Part 1: Understanding Yourself

Chapter 1: Self-Discovery and Personal Growth

- Identifying Your Values and Goals: Clarify what you want in life and in a partner.

- Building Self-Esteem and Confidence: Develop a strong sense of self-worth.

- Overcoming Past Relationship Baggage: Heal from past experiences to move forward.

- Developing a Positive Mindset: Cultivate a healthy and optimistic outlook.

Chapter 2: Emotional Intelligence

- Understanding Your Emotions: Gain insight into your emotional responses.

- Empathy and Understanding Others: Enhance your ability to connect with others.

- Managing Stress and Anxiety: Learn techniques to stay calm and centered.

- Developing Healthy Coping Mechanisms: Build resilience in the face of challenges.

Chapter 3: Defining Your Relationship Needs

- Identifying Your Relationship Goals: Determine what you want in a relationship.

- Understanding Your Love Languages: Discover how you give and receive love.

- Setting Boundaries and Expectations: Establish clear and healthy boundaries.

- Recognizing Red Flags and Deal Breakers: Know when to walk away.

Part 2: Communication Skills

Chapter 4: Basics of Effective Communication

- The Foundations of Communication: Master the essentials of good communication.

- Active Listening Techniques: Improve your listening skills for better conversations.

- Nonverbal Communication Cues: Understand body language and its impact.

- Navigating Difficult Conversations: Handle tough talks with ease.

Chapter 5: Enhancing Communication in Relationships

- Expressing Yourself Clearly: Articulate your thoughts and feelings effectively.

- Digital Communication Etiquette: Navigate online interactions with grace.

- Conflict Resolution Strategies: Resolve disagreements constructively.

- Apologizing and Forgiving: Heal and move forward from conflicts.

Part 3: Finding a Partner

Chapter 6: Modern Dating Landscape

- Online Dating and Apps: Navigate the world of digital dating.

- Traditional Dating Methods: Explore timeless ways to meet people.

- Navigating Social Media in Dating: Balance your online presence and dating life.

- Balancing Dating with Personal Life: Maintain harmony between love and life.

Chapter 7: Creating an Attractive Profile

- Crafting a Compelling Bio: Write a bio that stands out.

- Choosing the Right Photos: Select images that reflect your best self.

- Communicating Effectively Online: Make meaningful connections digitally.

- Safety Tips for Online Dating: Stay safe while meeting new people.

Chapter 8: Meeting People Offline

- Expanding Your Social Circle: Increase your opportunities to meet new people.

- Attending Social Events and Gatherings: Make the most of social opportunities.

- Approaching and Talking to Strangers: Overcome shyness and initiate conversations.

- Utilizing Mutual Connections: Leverage your network for introductions.

Chapter 9: The First Date

- Planning the Perfect First Date: Create a memorable and enjoyable experience.

- Making a Great First Impression: Present yourself confidently and authentically.

- Effective Communication on a Date: Keep the conversation flowing.

- Evaluating Compatibility: Assess if there's potential for a future together.

Part 4: Building a Relationship

Chapter 10: Early Stages of a Relationship

- Understanding the Honeymoon Phase: Enjoy and navigate the initial excitement.

- Setting the Foundation for Trust: Build trust from the beginning.

- Navigating Differences and Conflicts: Handle early challenges constructively.

- Establishing Healthy Communication Patterns: Develop good habits early on.

Chapter 11: Developing Trust and Intimacy

- The Importance of Trust in Relationships: Understand trust's vital role.

- Building Trust Over Time: Strengthen your bond through consistent actions.

- Developing Emotional and Physical Intimacy: Deepen your connection on all levels.

- Maintaining Boundaries and Respect: Respect each other's individuality.

Chapter 12: Deepening Connection

- Building Emotional Intimacy: Share your inner world with your partner.

- Exploring Physical Intimacy: Develop a fulfilling physical relationship.

- Shared Experiences and Activities: Create memories together.

- Maintaining Individuality within a Relationship: Balance closeness and independence.

Chapter 13: Long-Term Relationship Success

- Sustaining Love and Affection: Keep the romance alive.

- Effective Conflict Resolution: Navigate disputes without damage.

- Supporting Each Other's Growth: Encourage and inspire one another.

- Planning for the Future Together: Set goals and dreams as a couple.

Part 5: Advanced Relationship Dynamics

Chapter 14: Navigating Serious Commitments

- Moving In Together: Prepare for cohabitation.

- Engagement and Marriage: Take the next steps in your relationship.

- Blending Families and Parenting: Navigate complex family dynamics.

- Financial Planning and Shared Goals: Manage your finances as a team.

Chapter 15: Dealing with External Influences

- Managing Relationships with In-Laws: Maintain harmony with extended family.

- Balancing Friends and Your Relationship: Keep your friendships healthy.

- Handling Social Media and Privacy: Protect your relationship's privacy.

- Coping with Life Changes and Stress: Support each other through tough times.

Chapter 16: Specific Relationship Types

- Long-Distance Relationships: Maintain a strong connection across distances.

- Intercultural and Interfaith Relationships: Respect and blend diverse backgrounds.

- Relationships with Different Life Circumstances: Adapt to unique challenges.

Part 6: Enhancing and Sustaining Relationships

Chapter 17: Keeping the Spark Alive

- Planning Date Nights and Getaways: Prioritize time together.

- Exploring New Activities Together: Keep things exciting and fresh.

- Keeping Romance and Passion Alive: Maintain a loving and passionate connection.

- Surprising Each Other: Show your partner they are cherished.

Chapter 18: Personal Growth and Relationship Development

- Encouraging Each Other's Dreams: Support each other's ambitions.

- Continuing Education and Learning Together: Grow and learn as a couple.

- Supporting Each Other Through Changes: Navigate life's changes together.

- Celebrating Milestones and Achievements: Acknowledge and celebrate your journey.

Part 7: Endings and New Beginnings

Chapter 19: Recognizing When to End a Relationship

- Identifying Unhealthy Patterns: Recognize when things aren't working.

- Understanding When to Let Go: Accept when it's time to move on.

- Planning a Respectful Breakup: End things with dignity and respect.

- Healing and Moving Forward: Focus on recovery and growth.

Chapter 20: Rebuilding After a Breakup

- Self-Care and Healing: Prioritize your well-being.

- Learning from Past Relationships: Use past experiences to grow.

- Rebuilding Confidence and Trust: Regain your self-assurance.

- Opening Yourself to New Possibilities: Embrace new opportunities for love.

Chapter 21: New Beginnings

- Embracing Change and Growth: Welcome new beginnings.

- Rediscovering Yourself: Reconnect with who you are.

- Building a New Vision for the Future: Create a fresh outlook.

- Finding Love Again: Open your heart to new love.

Conclusion

- Reflect on your relationship journey.

- Continue to grow and learn.

Appendices

- Glossary of relationship terms.

- Recommended reading and resources.

- Worksheets and exercises.

- Contact information for relationship support services.

- About the publisher.

- Acknowledgments.

If you want to take control of your dating life and build meaningful connections, then this book is your essential guide. Packed with insights, strategies, and practical advice, "HowExpert Guide to Dating and Relationships" empowers you to create lasting, fulfilling relationships. Don't wait—start your journey to love and connection today!

Introduction

The Importance of Dating and Relationships

Dating and relationships are fundamental aspects of the human experience, deeply intertwined with our emotional, psychological, and physical well-being. They provide companionship, emotional support, and a sense of belonging that enrich our lives in profound ways. Understanding the dynamics of dating and relationships can lead to more fulfilling and meaningful connections, enhancing our overall quality of life. Here's an in-depth look at why dating and relationships are crucial and how they impact various facets of our existence:

1. Emotional Well-being

- Emotional Stability: Healthy relationships significantly contribute to our emotional stability and happiness.

- Safe Space: They offer a safe space to express our feelings, share our experiences, and receive emotional support.

- Stress Reduction: The presence of a loving partner can alleviate feelings of loneliness, reduce stress, and promote a sense of security and peace.

2. Personal Growth

- Comfort Zone: Relationships challenge us to grow, learn, and become better individuals.

- New Skills: They push us out of our comfort zones, encourage us to develop new skills, and help us gain a deeper understanding of ourselves.

- Valuable Lessons: Through relationships, we learn valuable lessons about empathy, patience, and compromise, which are essential for personal development.

3. Social Connection

- Community: Being in a relationship fosters a sense of community and social belonging.

- Social Network: It connects us to a broader social network, including friends, family, and community groups.

- Social Support: These connections can enhance our social life, provide support systems, and create a sense of inclusion and shared purpose.

4. Physical Health

- Health Outcomes: Studies consistently show that strong relationships can lead to better health outcomes.

- Lower Stress: Individuals in healthy relationships tend to have lower stress levels, stronger immune systems, and a longer lifespan.

- Healthier Choices: The emotional support provided by a partner can encourage healthier lifestyle choices, such as regular exercise, a balanced diet, and adherence to medical advice.

5. Life Satisfaction

- Sense of Purpose: A fulfilling relationship can significantly enhance overall life satisfaction.

- Positive Outlook: It provides a sense of purpose and meaning, contributing to a more positive outlook on life.

- Joy and Contentment: The joy and contentment derived from a loving relationship can permeate other areas of life, including work, hobbies, and personal aspirations.

Understanding these benefits underscores the importance of investing time and effort into developing and maintaining healthy relationships. By recognizing the profound impact that relationships have on our well-being, we can approach dating and relationships with greater intention and commitment.

How to Use This Guide for Maximum Benefit

To derive the most value from this guide, it's essential to approach it with a thoughtful and engaged mindset. Here are practical steps to ensure you maximize the benefits:

1. Read Sequentially

- Start and Progress: Begin at the start and progress through the chapters in order.

- Comprehensive Understanding: This guide is structured to build on previous sections, providing a comprehensive understanding of dating and relationships.

2. Reflect and Apply

- Reflect on Content: After reading each chapter, take time to reflect on the content.

- Practical Application: Consider how the concepts and strategies relate to your own experiences and relationships.

3. Stay Open-Minded

- New Ideas: Be receptive to new ideas and perspectives.

- Personal Growth: Some concepts may be unfamiliar or challenge your existing beliefs. Give them a fair chance.

4. Engage Actively

- Participate in Activities: Engage in the recommended activities and discussions.

- Reinforce Learning: Active engagement will reinforce your learning and help you internalize the concepts.

5. Revisit and Review

- Dynamic Relationships: Relationships are dynamic, and our needs and circumstances change over time.

- Periodic Review: Revisit the guide periodically to review key concepts and refresh your understanding.

By following these steps, you can ensure that you fully benefit from the insights and strategies provided in this guide. Embrace the journey with an open heart and a willingness to learn, and you'll be well on your way to building healthier and more fulfilling relationships.

Key Themes in Dating and Relationships

This guide is organized around several key themes that are essential for understanding and navigating dating and relationships. Each theme addresses specific aspects of relationships, providing a comprehensive framework for building and sustaining meaningful connections:

1. Self-Understanding

- Self-Discovery: Knowing yourself, including your values, goals, and emotional landscape, is the foundation of healthy relationships.

- Personal Growth: This theme covers self-discovery, personal growth, and emotional intelligence.

2. Communication

- Effective Communication: Effective communication is the cornerstone of any successful relationship.

- Key Skills: This theme explores active listening, conflict resolution, and digital communication etiquette.

3. Finding a Partner

- Modern Dating: Modern dating involves various methods and platforms.

- Practical Advice: This theme addresses creating an attractive profile, meeting people both online and offline, and planning successful first dates.

4. Building and Sustaining Relationships

- Trust and Intimacy: Building a strong relationship requires trust, intimacy, and shared experiences.

- Relationship Strategies: This theme delves into developing trust and intimacy, deepening connections, and maintaining long-term relationship success.

5. *Advanced Relationship Dynamics*

- Serious Commitments: As relationships evolve, they encounter new challenges and dynamics.

- Complex Scenarios: This theme covers navigating serious commitments, managing external influences, and handling specific relationship types.

6. *Enhancing and Sustaining Relationships*

- Continuous Effort: Keeping a relationship vibrant and fulfilling requires ongoing effort and personal growth.

- Relationship Investment: This theme includes keeping the spark alive, supporting each other's dreams, and celebrating milestones.

7. *Endings and New Beginnings*

- Recognizing Patterns: Recognizing when a relationship is no longer healthy and navigating breakups respectfully are crucial skills.

- Moving Forward: This theme addresses recognizing unhealthy patterns, healing after a breakup, and opening yourself to new possibilities.

By understanding and applying these key themes, you can navigate the complexities of dating and relationships with confidence and grace. This guide provides the knowledge and tools you need to create lasting, meaningful connections.

Conclusion of the Introduction

If you are ready to transform your dating life and build fulfilling relationships, then this guide is your essential companion. As you embark on this journey, remember that each step you take brings you closer to the love and connection you desire. Dive in, stay open, and let this guide lead you to a more enriched and satisfying relationship experience. Investing in your relationships is one of the most rewarding endeavors you can undertake, and this guide is here to support you every step of the way.

Part 1: Understanding Yourself

Chapter 1: Self-Discovery and Personal Growth

Understanding yourself is the cornerstone of building strong, healthy relationships. This chapter focuses on self-discovery and personal growth, providing you with the tools to identify your values, build self-esteem, overcome past relationship baggage, and develop a positive mindset. By investing in yourself, you create a solid foundation for successful relationships.

1.1 Identifying Your Values and Goals

Understanding your core values and goals is essential in forming a strong foundation for your relationships. Your values represent what is most important to you, while your goals outline what you aspire to achieve. Here are comprehensive steps to help you identify and align them effectively:

A. Reflect on Your Beliefs

1. Acknowledge Beliefs:

- Self-Reflection: Spend dedicated time thinking about the principles that guide your decisions and actions. These principles often stem from your upbringing, experiences, and intrinsic sense of right and wrong.

- Introspection Techniques: Use techniques like journaling, meditation, or quiet contemplation to dive deep into your core beliefs. This process allows you to gain insight into what truly matters to you.

2. Key Questions:

- Guiding Questions: Consider profound questions such as: What do I believe in? What core values drive my behavior? What principles will I never compromise on?

- Clarity and Insight: Reflecting on these questions can provide profound clarity on your values, helping you to articulate and prioritize them.

B. Assess Your Priorities

1. Determine Importance:

- Life Aspects: Identify the key areas of your life, such as family, career, friendships, health, and personal development. Each area holds different levels of importance for different individuals.

- Personal Reflection: Think deeply about how much time, energy, and resources you are willing to invest in each aspect. This will help you understand what you value most.

2. Rank Priorities:

- Prioritization Process: Rank these life aspects in order of importance to see where your primary focus lies.

- Alignment with Desires: This ranking process helps you ensure that your actions and decisions are aligned with your true desires, allowing you to live a life that is congruent with your deepest values.

C. Set Clear Goals

1. Define SMART Goals:

- Specific: Clearly define what you want to achieve in detail.

- Measurable: Establish criteria for measuring progress and success.

- Attainable: Ensure that your goals are realistic and achievable given your current resources and constraints.

- Relevant: Align your goals with your values and long-term vision.

- Time-bound: Set a clear deadline for achieving your goals to maintain focus and urgency.

2. Example Goal:

- Health Priority: If health is a core value, a specific goal might be to commit to exercising for at least 30 minutes, three times a week.

- Motivation and Direction: Such clear goals provide a sense of direction and intrinsic motivation, keeping you committed to your path.

D. Align Your Actions

1. Consistency:

- Daily Actions: Ensure that your everyday actions and decisions are a reflection of your values and goals. Consistency in your actions builds integrity and trust, both within yourself and in your relationships.

- Behavioral Alignment: Regularly ask yourself if your current actions are in line with your values. This helps you stay true to what you believe in, fostering a strong sense of self and purpose.

2. Regular Review:

- Goal Adjustment: Periodically review and adjust your goals to ensure they remain relevant and aligned with your evolving values and life circumstances.

- Self-Check: Conduct regular self-checks to ensure that you are on the right path. This involves reflecting on your progress, celebrating achievements, and making necessary adjustments to stay on track.

By following these comprehensive steps, you will create a solid framework for personal growth and relationship development. This foundation will not only support your individual journey but also enhance the quality and depth of your relationships, leading to a more fulfilling and purposeful life.

1.2 Building Self-Esteem and Confidence

High self-esteem and confidence are crucial for healthy relationships. They allow you to assert your needs and boundaries while fostering mutual respect. Here's how to build them:

A. Practice Self-Acceptance

1. Embrace Strengths:

- Recognition: Embrace your strengths and acknowledge your weaknesses without judgment. Recognize the unique qualities and talents you possess.

- Celebrate Uniqueness: Understand that your individuality is what makes you special. Focus on your positive attributes and how they contribute to your life and relationships.

2. Self-Acceptance:

- Imperfection Acceptance: Understand that nobody is perfect, and accept yourself as you are. Embrace your flaws as part of your unique character.

- Foundation of Self-Esteem: Self-acceptance is the foundation of self-esteem. By accepting yourself fully, you can build a strong sense of self-worth.

B. Challenge Negative Thoughts

1. Identify Negative Thoughts:

- Awareness: Identify self-critical thoughts and patterns. Pay attention to moments when you doubt yourself or feel inadequate.

- Thought Replacement: Replace negative thoughts with positive affirmations. Challenge the validity of your negative beliefs and consider more empowering alternatives.

2. Positive Affirmations:

- Reframe Beliefs: For example, if you think, "I'm not good enough," counter it with, "I am capable and worthy of love."

- Self-Talk: Positive self-talk can reshape your self-perception. Regularly affirm your strengths and capabilities to reinforce a positive self-image.

C. Set Achievable Goals

1. Small Goals:

- Incremental Steps: Accomplishing small goals boosts your confidence and motivates you to tackle larger challenges. Break down big tasks into manageable steps.

- Confidence Building: Each small success builds your confidence, demonstrating your ability to achieve your objectives.

2. Celebrate Successes:

- Acknowledgment: Celebrate your successes, no matter how small they may seem. Recognize and reward yourself for your efforts and achievements.

- Reinforcement: Achieving goals reinforces your belief in your abilities, fostering a stronger sense of self-efficacy.

D. Surround Yourself with Positive Influences

1. Supportive Environment:

- Uplifting Relationships: Spend time with people who uplift and support you. Positive relationships encourage growth and self-confidence.

- Healthy Connections: Engage with individuals who celebrate your successes and provide constructive feedback.

2. Avoid Negativity:

- Boundaries: Avoid those who bring negativity into your life. Set boundaries to protect your self-esteem from harmful influences.

- Positivity: A supportive environment nurtures confidence and self-esteem, creating a space for you to thrive.

E. Engage in Self-Care

1. Physical Well-Being:

- Health Focus: Take care of your physical, emotional, and mental well-being. Prioritize activities that enhance your overall health.

- Holistic Care: Regular exercise, a balanced diet, adequate sleep, and mental health practices contribute to your well-being.

2. Self-Care Activities:

- Joyful Engagement: Engage in activities that bring you joy and relaxation. Whether it's a hobby, a creative outlet, or simple relaxation, self-care boosts your mood and confidence.

- Routine: Incorporate self-care into your daily routine to maintain a healthy balance and reinforce your self-worth.

By following these strategies, you can build and maintain high self-esteem and confidence. These qualities are essential for fostering healthy relationships, as they enable you to set boundaries, communicate effectively, and engage with others from a place of self-respect and authenticity.

1.3 Overcoming Past Relationship Baggage

Past relationships can leave emotional scars that affect your current and future relationships. It's important to address and overcome this baggage to move forward effectively. Here's a comprehensive approach to help you heal and grow:

A. Acknowledge Your Feelings

1. Express Emotions:

- Emotional Release: Allow yourself to feel and express your emotions without suppression. Bottling up feelings can lead to unresolved issues that linger.

- Healthy Outlets: Find healthy outlets for expressing emotions, such as crying, writing, or talking to someone you trust. Emotional release is a crucial step towards healing.

2. Process Feelings:

- Journaling: Journaling can be a powerful tool for processing your feelings. Writing down your thoughts and emotions helps you understand and organize them.

- Talking: Discussing your feelings with a trusted friend, family member, or therapist can provide perspective and support. Verbalizing your emotions can make them more manageable.

B. Learn from Past Experiences

1. Reflect on the Past:

- Introspection: Reflect on past relationships to understand what went wrong and what you can do differently. This introspection helps you gain valuable insights.

- Self-Analysis: Consider the role you played in the relationship's dynamics and outcomes. Understanding your contributions can help you make positive changes.

2. Identify Patterns:

- Pattern Recognition: Identify patterns and behaviors in past relationships that may have contributed to their failure. Common patterns include poor communication, lack of trust, or repeated conflicts.

- Behavioral Changes: This reflection helps you pinpoint areas for improvement and change. By recognizing these patterns, you can avoid repeating the same mistakes in future relationships.

C. Seek Professional Help if Needed

1. Therapy:

- Counseling: Consider seeking therapy or counseling to help process your emotions and gain perspective. A professional can provide guidance and tools for healing.

- Emotional Support: Therapists can offer a safe space to explore deep-seated issues and work through them constructively.

2. Professional Support:

- Healing Facilitation: Professional support can facilitate deeper healing by addressing underlying emotional wounds and providing coping strategies.

- Personal Growth: Therapy can also promote personal growth and self-awareness, helping you build healthier relationships in the future.

D. Forgive Yourself and Others

1. Let Go of Grudges:

- Emotional Release: Let go of grudges and self-blame to free yourself from past burdens. Holding onto resentment can hinder your ability to move forward.

- Inner Peace: Release negative emotions by practicing forgiveness. This process can bring inner peace and emotional freedom.

2. Forgiveness:

- True Forgiveness: Understand that forgiveness does not mean forgetting or excusing past behavior. It means releasing the emotional hold that past pain has on you.

- Liberation: Forgiveness is a liberating act that allows you to move forward without the weight of past hurts. It opens the door to new, healthier relationships.

E. Create New Narratives

1. Positive Narratives:

- Reframe Experiences: Replace negative narratives about past relationships with positive ones. Focus on what you learned and how those experiences shaped you.

- Constructive Outlook: Emphasize personal growth and the positive aspects of past relationships, even if they ended badly. This constructive outlook promotes healing.

2. Focus on Growth:

- Learning and Growth: Focus on what you learned and how you grew from those experiences. Every relationship teaches valuable lessons that contribute to your personal development.

- Empowerment: By creating new, empowering narratives, you can transform past pain into a source of strength and wisdom. Positive narratives foster resilience and optimism.

By following these steps, you can effectively address and overcome past relationship baggage. This process not only heals old wounds but also prepares you for healthier, more fulfilling relationships in the future.

1.4 Developing a Positive Mindset

A positive mindset enhances your overall well-being and attracts healthy relationships. Cultivating this mindset involves the following steps:

A. Practicing Gratitude

1. Acknowledge Positives:

- Recognition: Regularly acknowledge and appreciate the good things in your life, no matter how small they may seem. This practice shifts your focus from what you lack to what you have.

- Daily Practice: Make it a habit to spend a few minutes each day reflecting on positive experiences and blessings.

2. Gratitude Journal:

- Documentation: Keep a gratitude journal to record daily instances of gratitude. Writing down positive experiences helps reinforce them in your mind.

- Reflection: Reviewing your journal regularly reminds you of the positives in your life, fostering a consistent positive outlook.

B. Maintaining Optimism

1. Positive Focus:

- Hopeful Outlook: Focus on potential positive outcomes rather than dwelling on negatives. This mindset encourages proactive and hopeful thinking.

- Solution-Oriented: When facing challenges, concentrate on finding solutions and opportunities for growth rather than fixating on problems.

2. Reframe Challenges:

- Growth Mindset: Reframe challenges as opportunities for growth and learning. View obstacles as stepping stones to personal development.

- Resilience: Optimism enhances resilience, enabling you to bounce back from setbacks with greater ease and confidence.

C. Engaging in Positive Self-Talk

1. Encourage Yourself:

- Self-Motivation: Encourage and motivate yourself with kind and constructive internal dialogue. Be your own cheerleader and recognize your efforts and achievements.

- Affirmations: Use positive affirmations to reinforce your self-worth and capabilities.

2. Replace Negative Thoughts:

- Thought Replacement: Replace self-defeating thoughts like "I can't do this" with empowering ones like "I can learn and improve."

- Self-Belief: Positive self-talk strengthens self-belief and fosters a can-do attitude.

D. Surrounding Yourself with Positivity

1. Positive Content:

- Inspiration: Engage with positive content, environments, and people. Consume media and literature that inspire and uplift you.

- Motivation: Listen to motivating podcasts, watch inspiring videos, and read uplifting books to maintain a positive mindset.

2. Uplifting Environment:

- Supportive Network: Surround yourself with people who uplift and support you. Build relationships with those who encourage your growth and happiness.

- Positive Spaces: Spend time in places that make you feel good and foster positivity.

E. Visualizing Success

1. Goal Visualization:

- Mental Imagery: Regularly visualize your goals and the successful outcomes you desire. Picture yourself achieving your aspirations vividly and in detail.

- Visualization Practice: Spend a few minutes each day visualizing success in various aspects of your life.

2. Motivation:

- Belief Enhancement: Visualization can enhance your motivation and belief in your ability to achieve your goals. Seeing your success in your mind's eye makes it feel more attainable.

- Action Orientation: Visualization turns dreams into achievable realities by aligning your mental focus with your actions.

F. Practicing Mindfulness and Meditation

1. Stay Present:

- Mindfulness: Practice mindfulness to stay present and reduce stress. Mindfulness involves being fully aware of your thoughts, feelings, and surroundings in the present moment.

- Meditation: Incorporate meditation into your routine to cultivate a sense of inner peace and clarity.

2. Emotional Stability:

- Stress Reduction: Mindfulness and meditation can help you manage negative emotions and maintain a balanced perspective. These practices promote emotional stability and resilience.

- Calmness: Regular meditation fosters a sense of calm and improves your ability to handle life's challenges with grace and composure.

By focusing on self-discovery and personal growth, you lay a solid foundation for healthier, more fulfilling relationships. This chapter equips you with the tools to understand yourself better, boost your self-esteem, and approach relationships with a positive and proactive mindset. This journey of self-discovery not only enhances your relationships but also contributes significantly to your overall personal development and happiness.

Chapter 1 Review: Self-Discovery and Personal Growth

Understanding yourself is crucial for building strong, healthy relationships. This chapter provides tools for self-discovery and personal growth, focusing on identifying values, building self-esteem, overcoming past relationship baggage, and developing a positive mindset.

1.1 Identifying Your Values and Goals

- Reflect on Beliefs: Spend time understanding the principles that guide your actions and decisions.

- Assess Priorities: Determine which aspects of life, such as family, career, friendships, health, and personal development, are most important to you.

- Set Clear Goals: Define specific, measurable, attainable, relevant, and time-bound (SMART) goals aligned with your values.

- Align Actions: Ensure your daily actions consistently reflect your values and goals. Regularly review and adjust your goals to stay on track.

1.2 Building Self-Esteem and Confidence

- Practice Self-Acceptance: Embrace your strengths and acknowledge your weaknesses without judgment. Accept yourself as you are.

- Challenge Negative Thoughts: Identify self-critical thoughts and replace them with positive affirmations, such as "I am capable and worthy of love."

- Set Achievable Goals: Start with small, manageable goals to build confidence and motivation. Celebrate each success, no matter how small.

- Surround with Positivity: Spend time with people who uplift and support you. Avoid those who bring negativity into your life.

- Engage in Self-Care: Prioritize your physical, emotional, and mental well-being by engaging in activities that bring you joy and fulfillment.

1.3 Overcoming Past Relationship Baggage

- Acknowledge Feelings: Allow yourself to feel and express your emotions without suppression. Journaling or talking with a trusted friend can help process these feelings.

- Learn from Experiences: Reflect on past relationships to understand what went wrong and what you can do differently. This helps identify patterns and behaviors to change.

- Seek Professional Help if Needed: Therapy or counseling can provide valuable tools for healing and offer an unbiased perspective on your experiences.

- Forgive Yourself and Others: Let go of grudges and self-blame to free yourself from past burdens. Forgiveness is about releasing the hold that past pain has on you.

- Create New Narratives: Replace negative narratives about past relationships with positive ones. Focus on what you learned and how you grew from those experiences.

1.4 Developing a Positive Mindset

- Practice Gratitude: Regularly acknowledge and appreciate the good things in your life. Keep a gratitude journal to remind yourself of these positives.

- Maintain Optimism: Focus on potential positive outcomes rather than dwelling on negatives. Reframe challenges as opportunities for growth and learning.

- Engage in Positive Self-Talk: Encourage and motivate yourself with kind and constructive internal dialogue. Replace thoughts like "I can't do this" with "I can learn and improve."

- Surround with Positivity: Engage with positive content, environments, and people. This includes reading uplifting books, listening to motivating podcasts, and spending time in places that make you feel good.

- Visualize Success: Regularly visualize your goals and the successful outcomes you desire. Visualization can enhance your motivation and belief in your ability to achieve your goals.

- Practice Mindfulness: Use mindfulness and meditation to stay present and reduce stress. These practices help manage negative emotions and maintain a balanced perspective.

By focusing on self-discovery and personal growth, you lay a solid foundation for healthier, more fulfilling relationships. This chapter equips you with the tools to understand yourself better, build self-esteem, and approach relationships with a positive and proactive mindset. This journey of self-discovery not only enhances your relationships but also contributes significantly to your overall personal development and happiness.

Chapter 2: Emotional Intelligence

Emotional intelligence (EI) is the ability to understand and manage your own emotions, as well as recognize and influence the emotions of others. It plays a crucial role in building healthy, fulfilling relationships. This chapter focuses on enhancing your EI through understanding your own emotions, developing empathy, managing stress, and adopting healthy coping mechanisms. By improving your emotional intelligence, you can navigate the complexities of relationships with greater ease and success.

2.1 Understanding Your Emotions

Emotional intelligence begins with a deep understanding of your own emotions. This self-awareness is the foundation upon which all other aspects of EI are built. It involves recognizing your feelings, understanding their origins, and assessing how they affect your thoughts and actions. Developing this self-awareness can lead to greater emotional stability and more fulfilling relationships. Here's how to cultivate a profound understanding of your emotions:

A. Identify Your Emotions

1. Acknowledge Emotions:

- Awareness: Start by paying close attention to your feelings throughout the day. Whenever you experience a strong emotion, take a moment to identify and name it (e.g., happy, sad, angry, frustrated). This practice helps in becoming more aware of your emotional state.

- Naming Emotions: Use specific labels for your emotions rather than general terms. For instance, distinguish between anger and frustration or between happiness and contentment.

2. *Understand Triggers:*

- Reflection: Reflect on what triggers specific emotions. Is it a person, situation, or thought pattern? By identifying triggers, you can gain insight into why you feel a certain way and address underlying issues.

- Pattern Recognition: Notice recurring triggers and patterns. This can help you anticipate and manage your emotional responses more effectively.

B. Analyze Impact

1. Behavioral Influence:

- Reaction Analysis: Consider how your emotions influence your behavior. Do certain feelings lead you to react impulsively, withdraw, or engage in specific actions? Understanding this can help you manage your reactions more effectively.

- Conscious Response: Aim to respond to your emotions thoughtfully rather than reacting impulsively. This conscious approach promotes emotional stability and healthier interactions.

2. Journaling:

- Daily Tracking: Keep a daily journal to track your emotions and their triggers. Write down how you felt, what caused those feelings, and how you reacted. This practice helps identify patterns and gain deeper insights into your emotional landscape.

- Reflection and Learning: Regularly review your journal entries to reflect on your emotional patterns and growth. Use these insights to make conscious changes in your behavior and emotional management.

C. Mindfulness Practice

1. Stay Present:

- Mindfulness Exercises: Engage in mindfulness exercises to stay present and connected with your emotions. Mindfulness involves observing your thoughts and feelings without judgment, which can help you understand and manage your emotions better.

- Breathing Techniques: Practice deep breathing techniques to center yourself and stay grounded in the present moment. This can help you stay calm and focused during emotional upheavals.

2. Emotional Regulation:

- Non-Judgmental Observation: Observe your emotions without labeling them as good or bad. This non-judgmental approach helps in accepting your emotions as they are, which is the first step towards managing them effectively.

- Meditation: Incorporate meditation into your routine to develop greater emotional awareness and regulation. Meditation fosters a deeper connection with your inner self and promotes emotional balance.

By following these steps, you can develop a profound understanding of your emotions. This self-awareness is crucial for building emotional intelligence, which in turn leads to more stable and fulfilling relationships. Understanding your emotions enables you to navigate your inner world with greater clarity and confidence, laying the foundation for a more emotionally balanced and connected life.

2.2 Empathy and Understanding Others

Empathy is the ability to understand and share the feelings of others, which is crucial for building strong and healthy relationships. Developing empathy involves more than just acknowledging others' emotions; it requires actively engaging with them. Here's how to enhance your empathy and understanding of others:

A. Active Listening

1. Full Attention:

- Engagement: Pay full attention when someone is speaking. Avoid distractions, such as looking at your phone or thinking about your response while they are talking.

- Nonverbal Signals: Show that you are engaged through nodding, maintaining eye contact, and using appropriate facial expressions. These signals indicate that you are fully present and attentive.

- Avoid Interrupting: Let the speaker finish their thoughts before you respond. This shows respect and gives you a better understanding of their message.

B. Ask Open-Ended Questions

1. Encourage Expression:

- Inquisitive Approach: Encourage others to express their feelings and experiences by asking open-ended questions that require more than a yes or no answer. For example, "How did that make you feel?" or "What was your experience like?"

- Deeper Understanding: These questions help you gain a deeper understanding of their emotional state and allow the speaker to share more comprehensive insights into their experiences.

2. Follow-Up Questions:

- Clarification: Ask follow-up questions to clarify points and show genuine interest. This demonstrates that you are engaged and eager to understand more deeply.

C. Reflect and Paraphrase

1. Show Understanding:

- Paraphrasing: Reflect back what the other person has said in your own words to show understanding and validate their feelings. For example, "It sounds like you felt really upset when that happened."

- Validation: This not only confirms that you are listening but also helps the speaker feel heard and valued. It can also help clarify any misunderstandings.

2. Emotional Validation:

- Acknowledge Feelings: Acknowledge the emotions expressed by the speaker. For instance, "I can see how that situation would be very frustrating for you."

D. Observe Nonverbal Cues

1. Body Language:

- Visual Cues: Pay attention to body language, facial expressions, and tone of voice to gain a fuller understanding of the other person's emotions. Nonverbal cues often reveal more than words alone.

- Inconsistencies: Be aware of inconsistencies between verbal and nonverbal messages. If someone says they are fine but their body language suggests otherwise, probe gently to understand their true feelings.

2. Contextual Understanding:

- Situational Awareness: Consider the context in which the conversation is taking place. The environment and circumstances can significantly impact emotions and reactions.

E. Put Yourself in Their Shoes

1. Perspective-Taking:

- Empathetic Imagination: Try to imagine how you would feel in the other person's situation. This perspective-taking enhances your ability to empathize genuinely and respond with compassion.

- Emotional Resonance: Aim to resonate with their emotional experience. This involves not only understanding their feelings but also connecting with them on an emotional level.

2. Compassionate Response:

- Supportive Actions: Respond in a way that shows compassion and support. Offer help or simply be present and acknowledge their feelings without trying to fix the problem immediately.

By developing these skills, you can enhance your empathy and understanding of others, leading to stronger, more meaningful relationships. Empathy allows you to connect deeply with others, foster trust, and create an environment where both you and others feel valued and understood.

2.3 Managing Stress and Anxiety

Stress and anxiety are common in relationships, and managing them effectively is key to maintaining emotional health. Here are practical strategies to help you manage stress and anxiety:

A. Identify Sources of Stress

1. Recognize Causes:

- Awareness: Take the time to recognize what causes stress in your life and relationships. Common sources include work pressures, financial concerns, unresolved conflicts, and lack of time.

- Specific Triggers: Identify specific situations or people that trigger stress. This understanding allows you to address the root causes rather than just the symptoms.

2. Stress Journaling:

- Documentation: Keep a stress journal to document situations that cause stress, how you feel, and your reactions. This can help you identify patterns and better understand your stress triggers.

B. Develop a Stress-Relief Routine

1. Daily Activities:

- Regular Exercise: Engage in physical activities such as walking, running, yoga, or any form of exercise you enjoy. Physical activity releases endorphins, which are natural stress relievers.

- Meditation and Mindfulness: Incorporate meditation and mindfulness practices into your daily routine. These activities help calm the mind and reduce anxiety.

- Hobbies: Dedicate time to hobbies and activities that you find relaxing and enjoyable. This can provide a mental break and reduce stress levels.

2. Relaxation Techniques:

- Techniques: Explore various relaxation techniques such as progressive muscle relaxation, guided imagery, or aromatherapy. Find what works best for you and make it a regular part of your routine.

C. Practice Deep Breathing

1. Calm Nervous System:

- Breathing Exercises: Engage in deep breathing exercises to calm your nervous system. A simple method is to inhale deeply through your nose, hold for a few seconds, and exhale slowly through your mouth.

- Consistent Practice: Practice deep breathing regularly, especially during stressful moments. This can quickly reduce feelings of stress and anxiety and help you regain control.

2. Breathing Techniques:

- 4-7-8 Technique: Try the 4-7-8 breathing technique: inhale for 4 seconds, hold for 7 seconds, and exhale for 8 seconds. This technique can promote relaxation and improve focus.

D. Time Management

1. Prioritize Tasks:

- Task Management: Prioritize tasks and set realistic goals to manage your time effectively. Use tools like to-do lists, planners, or digital apps to keep track of tasks and deadlines.

- Break Tasks: Break tasks into smaller, manageable steps to prevent feelings of overwhelm and enhance productivity.

2. Avoid Procrastination:

- Plan Ahead: Plan your day ahead of time and allocate specific time slots for each task. This reduces last-minute rushes and helps you stay organized.

- Set Boundaries: Learn to say no to additional responsibilities when you are already stretched thin. Setting boundaries protects your time and reduces stress.

E. Seek Support

1. Talk About Stressors:

- Communication: Talk to friends, family, or a professional therapist about your stressors. Sharing your concerns can provide relief, new perspectives, and practical solutions.

- Support Network: Build a support network of people who understand and can provide emotional support. Sometimes, just knowing you have someone to talk to can significantly reduce stress.

2. Professional Help:

- Therapy: Consider seeking professional help if stress and anxiety become overwhelming. Therapists can provide coping strategies and tools to manage stress effectively.

- Support Groups: Join support groups where you can share experiences and learn from others facing similar challenges.

By implementing these strategies, you can manage stress and anxiety more effectively, leading to better emotional health and more fulfilling relationships. Managing stress is not only about reducing immediate discomfort but also about creating a sustainable approach to maintaining balance and well-being in your daily life.

2.4 Developing Healthy Coping Mechanisms

Healthy coping mechanisms are essential for dealing with emotional challenges in a constructive way. Developing these skills can improve your emotional resilience and overall well-being. Here are some strategies:

A. Positive Self-Talk

1. Encourage Yourself:

- Affirmations: Replace negative thoughts with positive affirmations. Use phrases like "I can handle this," "I am strong," or "I am capable." These affirmations can help reframe your mindset and boost your confidence.

- Internal Dialogue: Continuously practice positive self-talk, especially during challenging situations. Positive self-talk can enhance your resilience and help you face difficulties with a more optimistic outlook.

2. Self-Compassion:

- Kindness to Self: Treat yourself with the same kindness and understanding you would offer a friend. Recognize that everyone makes mistakes and experiences setbacks, and be gentle with yourself during tough times.

B. Physical Activity

1. Exercise Regularly:

- Endorphin Boost: Regular exercise releases endorphins, which are natural mood enhancers. Engage in physical activities you enjoy, such as running, swimming, dancing, or yoga.

- Routine: Incorporate physical activity into your daily routine to maintain consistent benefits. Aim for at least 30 minutes of exercise most days of the week.

2. Stress Reduction:

- Active Stress Relief: Physical activity is a powerful way to reduce stress and improve mental health. Activities like walking in nature, playing sports, or even gardening can provide both physical and emotional benefits.

C. Creative Outlets

1. Express Emotions:

- Artistic Expression: Engage in creative activities like drawing, painting, writing, or playing music to express and manage your emotions. These outlets can be therapeutic and provide a constructive way to process feelings.

- Therapeutic Writing: Keep a journal where you can freely write about your thoughts and emotions. This practice can help you gain insights into your feelings and develop healthier coping mechanisms.

2. Innovation and Problem-Solving:

- Creative Problem-Solving: Use creativity to approach challenges from new perspectives. Think outside the box and develop innovative solutions to problems, which can enhance your problem-solving skills and reduce stress.

D. Problem-Solving Skills

1. Approach Challenges:

- Analytical Thinking: Approach challenges with a problem-solving mindset. Break down issues into smaller, manageable parts, and analyze each component.

- Action Plan: Identify the issue, brainstorm possible solutions, and take actionable steps. Effective problem-solving can reduce stress and increase confidence.

2. Decision-Making:

- Informed Choices: Make informed decisions by gathering information, weighing pros and cons, and considering potential outcomes. This approach can help you feel more in control and less anxious about challenges.

E. Healthy Lifestyle Choices

1. Balanced Living:

- Nutrition: Maintain a balanced diet rich in fruits, vegetables, whole grains, and lean proteins. Proper nutrition supports both physical and emotional health.

- Sleep: Ensure you get adequate sleep each night, aiming for 7-9 hours. Good sleep is crucial for emotional stability and cognitive function.

2. Substance Management:

- Moderation: Avoid excessive consumption of alcohol, caffeine, and other substances that can negatively impact your mood and overall health. Opt for healthier alternatives and moderation.

F. Relaxation Techniques

1. Reduce Stress:

- Yoga: Practice yoga to combine physical movement with mindfulness and deep breathing. Yoga can enhance flexibility, reduce stress, and improve overall well-being.

- Meditation: Engage in meditation to quiet the mind and reduce stress. Even a few minutes of meditation each day can have significant benefits for emotional resilience.

2. Progressive Muscle Relaxation:

- Technique: Practice progressive muscle relaxation by tensing and then slowly releasing different muscle groups in your body. This technique can help reduce physical tension and promote relaxation.

3. Breathing Exercises:

- Calming Effects: Incorporate breathing exercises into your routine. Techniques like deep breathing, diaphragmatic breathing, or the 4-7-8 method can quickly calm your nervous system and reduce anxiety.

By incorporating these healthy coping mechanisms into your daily life, you can improve your emotional resilience and overall well-being. These strategies will help you manage stress, navigate challenges, and maintain a positive outlook, enhancing both your personal and relational happiness.

Chapter 2 Review: Emotional Intelligence

Emotional intelligence (EI) is crucial for building healthy, fulfilling relationships. This chapter focuses on enhancing your EI through understanding your own emotions, developing empathy, managing stress, and adopting healthy coping mechanisms. By improving your emotional intelligence, you can navigate the complexities of relationships with greater ease and success.

2.1 Understanding Your Emotions

- Identify Your Emotions: Pay close attention to your feelings and name them (e.g., happy, sad, angry). This practice increases awareness of your emotional state.

- Understand Triggers: Reflect on what triggers specific emotions, whether it's a person, situation, or thought pattern. This helps address underlying issues.

- Analyze Impact: Consider how your emotions influence your behavior and manage reactions more effectively.

- Journaling: Keep a daily journal to track your emotions and their triggers, helping identify patterns and gain insights.

- Mindfulness Practice: Engage in mindfulness exercises to stay present and connected with your emotions without judgment.

2.2 Empathy and Understanding Others

- Active Listening: Pay full attention when someone is speaking, avoid interrupting, and show engagement through nodding and eye contact.

- Ask Open-Ended Questions: Encourage others to express their feelings by asking questions that require more than yes or no answers.

- Reflect and Paraphrase: Reflect back what the other person has said in your own words to show understanding and validate their feelings.

- Observe Nonverbal Cues: Pay attention to body language, facial expressions, and tone of voice to understand the other person's emotions.

- Put Yourself in Their Shoes: Imagine how you would feel in the other person's situation to enhance genuine empathy and compassion.

2.3 Managing Stress and Anxiety

- Identify Sources of Stress: Recognize what causes stress in your life and relationships, such as work pressures or unresolved conflicts.

- Develop a Stress-Relief Routine: Create a daily routine with activities like exercise, meditation, or hobbies to reduce stress.

- Practice Deep Breathing: Use deep breathing exercises to calm your nervous system and quickly reduce feelings of stress and anxiety.

- Time Management: Prioritize tasks, set realistic goals, and break tasks into smaller steps to prevent overwhelm and enhance productivity.

- Seek Support: Talk to friends, family, or a professional therapist about your stressors for relief, new perspectives, and practical solutions.

2.4 Developing Healthy Coping Mechanisms

- Positive Self-Talk: Replace negative thoughts with positive affirmations to boost confidence and resilience.

- Physical Activity: Engage in regular exercise to improve mood and reduce stress.

- Creative Outlets: Use creative activities like drawing, writing, or playing music to express and manage emotions.

- Problem-Solving Skills: Approach challenges with a problem-solving mindset, identify issues, brainstorm solutions, and take actionable steps.

- Healthy Lifestyle Choices: Maintain a balanced diet, get adequate sleep, and avoid excessive alcohol or caffeine consumption to support overall well-being.

- Relaxation Techniques: Practice relaxation techniques such as yoga, meditation, or progressive muscle relaxation to reduce stress and enhance emotional resilience.

Summary

Emotional intelligence is a cornerstone of healthy relationships. By understanding and managing your own emotions, empathizing with others, handling stress effectively, and developing healthy coping mechanisms, you can navigate the emotional complexities of relationships with greater ease and success. This chapter provides essential tools and practices to enhance your emotional intelligence, fostering stronger and more fulfilling connections with others. As you continue to develop your emotional intelligence, you'll find that your relationships become more harmonious, supportive, and deeply satisfying.

Chapter 3: Defining Your Relationship Needs

Establishing a clear understanding of your relationship needs is vital for creating and maintaining a healthy and fulfilling partnership. This chapter guides you through identifying your relationship goals, understanding your love languages, setting boundaries and expectations, and recognizing red flags and deal breakers. By defining what you need and want in a relationship, you can build a strong foundation for a successful and satisfying connection.

3.1 Identifying Your Relationship Goals

Identifying your relationship goals is the first step toward finding and maintaining a healthy, fulfilling relationship. Clear goals help you understand what you want and need from a partner and a relationship. Here's how to identify your relationship goals:

A. Reflect on Past Relationships

1. Evaluate Successes and Failures:

- Analyze Fulfillment: Reflect on why certain relationships were fulfilling and why others fell short. Identify the factors that contributed to your happiness or dissatisfaction in these relationships.

- Lessons Learned: Consider what you learned from each relationship. Understanding past experiences can guide you toward better choices in the future.

2. Identify Patterns:

- Recurring Themes: Look for recurring themes in your relationships. Are there certain qualities in partners that consistently lead to happiness or dissatisfaction?

- Behavioral Patterns: Recognize your own behaviors that have impacted past relationships, both positively and negatively.

B. Determine What You Want in a Partner

1. Core Values:

- Non-Negotiables: Identify non-negotiable values such as honesty, kindness, integrity, or ambition. These values form the foundation of a strong relationship.

- Alignment: Ensure your core values align with those of your potential partner to foster mutual respect and understanding.

2. Interests and Hobbies:

- Shared Interests: Consider shared interests that can strengthen your bond. Having common hobbies can enhance your connection and provide opportunities for quality time together.

- Complementary Activities: Also, appreciate complementary interests that allow for personal growth and new experiences.

3. Personality Traits:

- Desirable Traits: Think about the traits that you find appealing or necessary in a partner, such as humor, empathy, resilience, or patience.

- Compatibility: Assess how these traits complement your own personality and contribute to a harmonious relationship.

C. Consider Long-Term vs. Short-Term Goals

1. Short-Term Goals:

- Immediate Desires: What do you want to experience in the next few months or years? Consider whether you are interested in casual dating, exploring different types of relationships, or focusing on personal growth.

- Flexibility: Be open to evolving these goals as you gain more clarity about your preferences and experiences.

2. Long-Term Goals:

- Future Vision: Where do you see yourself in five or ten years? Consider your long-term aspirations such as marriage, family, or a long-term companionship.

- Life Plan Integration: Ensure your long-term relationship goals align with your overall life plan, including career and personal ambitions.

D. Align Goals with Personal Values

1. Life Aspirations:

- Holistic View: Consider how your career, lifestyle, and personal aspirations intersect with your relationship goals. Ensure that your relationship supports your broader life goals.

- Growth Support: Look for a partner whose goals and values support and enhance your personal growth and aspirations.

2. Mutual Support:

- Reciprocity: Ensure that your goals support each other's growth and aspirations. A healthy relationship involves mutual encouragement and support.

E. Visualize Your Ideal Relationship

1. Daily Interactions:

- Routine Life: Visualize how you and your partner interact daily. Consider the daily routines, habits, and rituals that define your ideal relationship.

- Quality Time: Think about how you spend quality time together, balancing personal time and together time.

2. Conflict Resolution:

- Communication Styles: Imagine how you handle conflicts. What communication styles and problem-solving approaches do you use? Healthy conflict resolution is essential for long-term relationship success.

- Resolution Techniques: Visualize constructive ways to navigate disagreements, ensuring that both partners feel heard and respected.

3. Support Systems:

- Emotional Support: Think about how you support each other's goals and dreams. Visualize the ways in which you provide emotional and practical support to each other.

- Shared Goals: Consider shared goals and how you work together to achieve them, fostering a sense of partnership and collaboration.

F. Write Down Your Goals

1. Specific Goals:

- Detailed Clarity: Write clear, specific goals that detail what you seek in a relationship. These goals should be tangible and actionable, providing a roadmap for your relationship journey.

- Measurable: Ensure that your goals are measurable, allowing you to track progress and make adjustments as needed.

2. Regular Review:

- Periodic Updates: Periodically review and update your goals to reflect your evolving needs and experiences. As you grow and change, your relationship goals should adapt accordingly.

- Reflective Practice: Use this review process as an opportunity for self-reflection and to ensure that your relationship remains aligned with your values and aspirations.

By identifying and clearly articulating your relationship goals, you set the stage for a more intentional and fulfilling relationship. This clarity helps you make informed decisions about potential partners and navigate your relationships with purpose and direction.

3.2 Understanding Your Love Languages

Understanding your love languages is vital for communicating love and affection effectively in a relationship. The concept of love languages, introduced by Dr. Gary Chapman, identifies five primary ways people express and receive love:

A. Words of Affirmation

1. Compliments and Praise:

- Expressions of Appreciation: Simple expressions of appreciation, such as "You did a great job" or "I love how you handled that," can be very meaningful. Verbal affirmations can uplift and reinforce positive feelings.

- Positive Feedback: Regularly providing positive feedback and acknowledging your partner's efforts can strengthen their confidence and emotional well-being.

2. Encouraging Words:

- Supportive Statements: Use words to offer support and encouragement. Statements like "I believe in you" or "You can do this" can be incredibly motivating.

- Affirmations: Incorporate affirmations into your daily conversations to continually express your love and appreciation.

B. Acts of Service

1. Helping Hand:

- Everyday Tasks: Everyday tasks like cooking dinner, running errands, or doing household chores can be significant gestures of love. These acts show that you are willing to take on responsibilities to ease your partner's burden.

- Supportive Actions: Volunteering to help with tasks, especially during stressful times, demonstrates your care and commitment.

2. Thoughtful Actions:

- Small Acts of Kindness: Small acts of kindness, like making coffee in the morning or taking care of a specific chore, show that you are attentive to your partner's needs and preferences.

- Planning and Preparation: Thoughtful actions that require planning, such as organizing a special date or preparing a favorite meal, can deeply convey your love.

C. Receiving Gifts

1. Meaningful Gifts:

- Thoughtful Gestures: Gifts that reflect thought and effort, such as a handmade item or a carefully chosen present, are particularly cherished. The significance lies in the thoughtfulness and the effort behind the gift.

- Personalized Gifts: Personalized gifts that cater to your partner's interests and preferences can strengthen your bond.

2. Special Occasions:

- Celebrating Milestones: Celebrating milestones like anniversaries, birthdays, or achievements with thoughtful gifts can reinforce your connection and show that you value these moments.

- Surprise Gifts: Unexpected gifts, even small ones, can also add excitement and joy to the relationship.

D. Quality Time

1. Focused Attention:

- Undivided Attention: Quality conversations and activities where you are fully present and engaged are crucial. This means setting aside distractions and focusing entirely on your partner.

- Active Listening: Listen actively and attentively to your partner during conversations, showing that you value their thoughts and feelings.

2. Shared Experiences:

- Enjoying Hobbies Together: Enjoying hobbies or activities together, such as hiking, cooking, or attending events, can enhance your connection and create lasting memories.

- Routine Quality Time: Make it a habit to regularly spend quality time together, whether it's a weekly date night or daily moments of connection.

E. Physical Touch

1. Affectionate Touch:

- Regular Affection: Regular physical affection, like cuddling, holding hands, hugging, or kissing, fosters intimacy and closeness.

- Physical Connection: Simple gestures like a gentle touch on the arm or a loving embrace can convey deep affection and reassurance.

2. Comfort and Reassurance:

- During Difficult Times: Physical touch during difficult times, such as a hug or a comforting hand on the back, can provide significant comfort and support, reinforcing your presence and care.

F. To Understand Your Love Language:

1. Take the Love Languages Quiz:

- Self-Assessment: Reflect on how you feel most appreciated and loved in relationships by taking the Love Languages Quiz. This can provide insights into your primary love language.

2. Reflect on Past Relationships:

- Analyze Experiences: Look at patterns in past relationships to see what made you feel valued and connected. Consider which gestures or actions from partners had the most positive impact on you.

3. Communicate with Your Partner:

- Mutual Understanding: Share your love languages with your partner and ask about theirs. This knowledge can enhance your relationship by ensuring both partners feel loved in the way they prefer.

- Implementation: Actively incorporate your partner's love language into your daily interactions to strengthen your bond and mutual understanding.

By understanding and applying the concept of love languages, you can improve communication and deepen the emotional connection in your relationship. This mutual understanding fosters a more supportive, affectionate, and fulfilling partnership.

3.3 Setting Boundaries and Expectations

Setting boundaries and expectations is essential for a healthy relationship. Boundaries define what you are comfortable with, and expectations outline what you hope to achieve together. Here's how to establish them effectively:

A. Identify Your Boundaries

1. Personal Space:

- Self-Care Needs: Determine your need for personal space and time. Understand what activities or alone time you require to recharge and maintain your well-being.

- Physical Boundaries: Define your comfort level regarding physical proximity and personal space in various situations.

2. Emotional Boundaries:

- Emotional Safety: Consider what emotional boundaries you need to feel secure. This includes how much emotional vulnerability you are comfortable sharing and receiving.

- Support Needs: Identify the type and amount of emotional support you need from your partner.

3. Digital Boundaries:

- Online Interaction: Establish limits on digital communication and social media. This includes how often you communicate online, what information you share, and your comfort level with public displays of your relationship.

- Privacy: Define what aspects of your digital life you prefer to keep private versus what you are comfortable sharing with your partner.

B. Communicate Clearly

1. Open Dialogue:

- Honest Communication: Discuss your boundaries and expectations openly with your partner. Be honest about what you need and why it's important to you.

- Initial Conversations: Have these conversations early in the relationship to set a clear foundation.

2. Active Listening:

- Attentive Listening: Listen attentively to your partner's needs and respect their boundaries. Show that you value their feelings and concerns.

- Validation: Validate their feelings and acknowledge their boundaries to build trust and mutual respect.

3. Clear Expression:

- Specificity: Be specific about your boundaries and expectations. Use clear, direct language to avoid misunderstandings.

C. Be Respectful and Considerate

1. Mutual Respect:

- Respect Differences: Ensure that both partners feel heard and respected. Recognize that your partner's boundaries and expectations may differ from yours and respect those differences.

- Empathy: Approach your partner's boundaries with empathy and understanding.

2. Adaptability:

- Flexibility: Be willing to adjust boundaries as the relationship evolves. Understand that needs and comfort levels can change over time.

- Compromise: Find a balance that respects both partners' needs without compromising individual comfort and security.

D. Revisit and Adjust

1. Periodic Review:

- Regular Check-Ins: Schedule regular discussions to revisit and adjust boundaries and expectations as needed. This ensures that both partners are still comfortable and aligned as the relationship progresses.

- Feedback Loop: Encourage open feedback about what's working and what needs adjustment.

2. Growth Consideration:

- Life Changes: Consider life changes and external factors that might require boundary adjustments. Be proactive in addressing these changes together.

E. Handle Conflicts Constructively

1. Calm Resolution:

- Stay Calm: Approach conflicts with a calm and constructive mindset. Avoid reacting impulsively and strive to remain composed.

- Constructive Dialogue: Use "I" statements to express your feelings without blaming your partner. For example, say, "I feel overwhelmed when we don't have alone time" instead of "You never give me space."

2. Solution-Focused:

- Collaborative Approach: Work together to find solutions that respect both partners' boundaries. Focus on finding common ground and mutually beneficial resolutions.

- Problem-Solving: Engage in problem-solving techniques such as brainstorming possible solutions and evaluating them together.

3. Conflict Management:

- Effective Strategies: Develop effective conflict management strategies, such as taking breaks during heated discussions to cool down and revisit the topic later with a clearer mind.

- Seeking Help: If needed, seek the help of a relationship counselor to navigate persistent conflicts and improve communication.

By identifying, communicating, and respecting boundaries and expectations, you create a foundation of trust and understanding in your relationship. Regularly revisiting these boundaries and handling conflicts constructively ensures that both partners feel secure and valued, contributing to a healthier and more fulfilling relationship.

3.4 Recognizing Red Flags and Deal Breakers

Recognizing red flags and deal breakers is crucial for protecting yourself and ensuring a healthy relationship. Red flags are warning signs that something might be wrong, while deal breakers are behaviors or traits that are unacceptable to you. Here's how to identify them:

A. Identify Your Non-Negotiables

1. Core Values:

- Essential Values: Identify non-negotiable values and behaviors that are essential for a healthy relationship, such as honesty, respect, loyalty, and mutual support.

- Personal Integrity: Ensure that these core values align with your personal integrity and long-term relationship goals.

2. Deal Breakers:

- Unacceptable Behaviors: List behaviors or traits that are unacceptable under any circumstances, such as infidelity, abuse (verbal, emotional, or physical), substance abuse, and dishonesty.

- Firm Boundaries: Establish clear boundaries around these deal breakers to protect your well-being and maintain a healthy relationship dynamic.

B. Be Aware of Common Red Flags

1. Lack of Communication:

- Communication Issues: Poor or inconsistent communication can indicate deeper issues in the relationship, such as avoidance, lack of interest, or emotional unavailability.

- Open Dialogue: Prioritize open and honest communication to address and resolve potential issues early on.

2. Controlling Behavior:

- Control Dynamics: If your partner tries to control your actions, decisions, or interactions with others, it's a significant red flag. This behavior can lead to manipulation and emotional abuse.

- Autonomy: Ensure that both partners maintain their autonomy and respect each other's independence.

3. *Disrespect:*

- Respectful Interaction: Any form of disrespect, whether verbal, emotional, or physical, is unacceptable. Disrespect can erode trust and create a toxic environment.

- Mutual Respect: Foster a relationship built on mutual respect and appreciation.

4. *Inconsistency:*

- Reliability: If your partner's actions don't match their words, it could be a sign of unreliability and lack of commitment.

- Consistency: Look for consistent behavior that aligns with stated intentions and commitments.

5. *Excessive Jealousy:*

- Jealousy Levels: While some jealousy is normal, excessive jealousy can be a sign of insecurity, possessiveness, and control issues.

- Healthy Trust: Build a relationship based on trust and security, where both partners feel valued and respected.

C. Trust Your Intuition

1. Intuitive Awareness:

- Gut Feelings: Pay attention to your gut feelings about your partner's behavior and the relationship. Your intuition can provide valuable insights into potential issues.

- Inner Voice: Trust your inner voice if something feels off or uncomfortable. Don't ignore or rationalize away these feelings.

D. Seek External Perspectives

1. Outside Opinions:

- Trusted Advice: Seek advice and perspectives from those you trust, such as friends, family, or a therapist. They can provide an objective viewpoint and help you gain clarity on your relationship.

- Different Perspectives: Consider different perspectives to ensure you are seeing the relationship from multiple angles and not missing any red flags.

2. Support System:

- Emotional Support: Lean on your support system for emotional support and guidance, especially when dealing with complex or challenging relationship issues.

E. Take Action

1. Proactive Steps:

- Address Issues: Address issues head-on and communicate your concerns directly with your partner. Honest dialogue is key to resolving conflicts and addressing red flags.

- Decision-Making: Make decisions that prioritize your well-being. If a red flag or deal breaker is identified, take the necessary steps to protect yourself, even if it means ending the relationship.

2. *Self-Advocacy:*

- Assertiveness: Be assertive in standing up for your needs and boundaries. Don't compromise your values or well-being to accommodate unacceptable behavior.

Chapter 3 Review: Defining Your Relationship Needs

Understanding your relationship needs is crucial for creating and maintaining a healthy and fulfilling partnership. This chapter guides you through identifying your relationship goals, understanding your love languages, setting boundaries and expectations, and recognizing red flags and deal breakers.

3.1 Identifying Your Relationship Goals

- Reflect on Past Relationships: Analyze what worked and what didn't to understand your needs and preferences. Identify patterns and key factors that contributed to your happiness or dissatisfaction.

- Determine What You Want in a Partner: List qualities that are important to you, such as core values, interests, personality traits, and lifestyle choices.

- Consider Long-Term vs. Short-Term Goals: Define goals for both short-term dating and long-term commitments, like marriage or family.

- Align Goals with Personal Values: Ensure your relationship goals match your personal values and life aspirations.

- Visualize Your Ideal Relationship: Imagine daily interactions, conflict resolution, and mutual support in your ideal relationship.

- Write Down Your Goals: Document and periodically review your relationship goals to keep them clear and updated.

3.2 Understanding Your Love Languages

Understanding love languages helps in expressing and receiving love effectively. The five primary love languages are:

- Words of Affirmation: Valuing verbal expressions of love, appreciation, and encouragement.

- Acts of Service: Feeling loved when your partner helps with tasks or does thoughtful actions.

- Receiving Gifts: Appreciating thoughtful and meaningful gifts that show you are valued.

- Quality Time: Valuing undivided attention and meaningful time spent together.

- Physical Touch: Feeling loved through physical closeness and affectionate touch.

To identify your love language:

- Take the Love Languages Quiz: Discover your primary love language.

- Reflect on Past Relationships: Consider how you've felt most loved in the past.

- Communicate with Your Partner: Discuss your love languages to understand each other's preferences and enhance your relationship.

3.3 Setting Boundaries and Expectations

Setting boundaries and expectations ensures a healthy relationship. Here's how:

- Identify Your Boundaries: Determine what makes you feel safe and respected, including physical, emotional, and digital boundaries.

- Communicate Clearly: Discuss boundaries and expectations openly with your partner to prevent misunderstandings.

- Be Respectful and Considerate: Respect each other's boundaries and understand that both partners have different needs.

- Revisit and Adjust: Regularly check and update boundaries and expectations as the relationship evolves.

- Handle Conflicts Constructively: Address issues calmly and find mutually respectful solutions when boundaries are breached.

3.4 Recognizing Red Flags and Deal Breakers

Identifying red flags and deal breakers is essential for a healthy relationship. Here's how:

- Identify Your Non-Negotiables: List absolute deal breakers and essential values, such as honesty, respect, and shared goals.

- Be Aware of Common Red Flags: Watch for signs like poor communication, controlling behavior, disrespect, inconsistency, and excessive jealousy.

- Trust Your Intuition: Address concerns early if something feels off to prevent bigger issues.

- Seek External Perspectives: Get insights and advice from trusted friends or family members.

- Take Action: Prioritize your well-being and address issues directly, even if it means ending the relationship.

Summary

Defining your relationship needs is a foundational step towards a healthy and fulfilling relationship. By identifying goals, understanding love languages, setting boundaries, and recognizing red flags, you can build a respectful and supportive partnership aligned with your values and goals. This approach ensures a clear path to a successful and satisfying relationship.

Chapter 4: Basics of Effective Communication

Communication is the bedrock of any healthy and successful relationship. It allows partners to share their thoughts, feelings, and needs effectively, fostering understanding and connection. This chapter delves into the fundamentals of effective communication, including clarity, honesty, respect, and empathy. It also covers essential skills such as active listening, understanding nonverbal cues, and navigating difficult conversations. Mastering these basics will enhance your ability to connect with others and build stronger, more supportive relationships.

4.1 The Foundations of Communication

Effective communication is the cornerstone of any healthy relationship. It involves the clear and open exchange of thoughts, feelings, and information. Understanding the foundations of communication can help you build stronger, more fulfilling connections with your partner. Here are the key components:

A. Clarity and Conciseness

1. Avoid Jargon:

- Simple Language: Use language that is easily understood by both parties to prevent misunderstandings. Avoid technical terms, slang, or jargon that might confuse your partner.

- Common Understanding: Ensure both partners have a common understanding of the terms and phrases used during conversations.

2. *Get to the Point:*

- Focused Communication: Avoid rambling and stay focused on the main message to keep the conversation clear and concise. Being direct helps in conveying your thoughts more effectively.

- Essential Details: Stick to the essential details that are relevant to the discussion, ensuring the conversation remains productive and on-topic.

B. Honesty and Openness

1. Share Your True Feelings:

- Emotional Honesty: Don't hide your emotions or opinions for fear of conflict. Open communication leads to a stronger bond and mutual understanding.

- Vulnerability: Allow yourself to be vulnerable by sharing your true feelings, which fosters intimacy and trust.

2. Transparency:

- Clear Intentions: Be transparent about your intentions and feelings to avoid misunderstandings. Clearly express your needs, desires, and concerns.

- Authenticity: Ensure that your words align with your true thoughts and feelings, maintaining authenticity in your communication.

C. Respect and Empathy

1. Validate Emotions:

- Acknowledge Feelings: Acknowledge your partner's feelings even if you don't agree with them. Validation shows that you respect their emotions and perspectives.

- Active Listening: Listen actively without interrupting, showing that you value what your partner has to say.

2. Show Compassion:

- Empathetic Responses: Demonstrate understanding and concern for your partner's emotional state. Use phrases like, "I can see why you feel that way" or "That sounds really tough."

- Supportive Actions: Offer support and comfort, reinforcing your empathy through actions as well as words.

D. Feedback and Reflection

1. Constructive Criticism:

- Helpful Feedback: Offer feedback in a way that is helpful and not hurtful. Focus on specific behaviors rather than personal attributes.

- Positive Framing: Frame your feedback positively, emphasizing what can be improved rather than just pointing out flaws.

2. Self-Reflection:

- Assess Communication Habits: Regularly assess and improve your own communication habits. Reflect on how your words and actions affect your partner.

- Continuous Improvement: Strive for continuous improvement in your communication skills, seeking to be more effective and empathetic.

E. Timing and Context

1. Find the Right Moment:

- Appropriate Timing: Ensure both parties are calm and available to talk. Avoid bringing up serious issues during stressful or busy times.

- Readiness: Check if your partner is ready and willing to engage in the conversation.

2. Private Setting:

- Comfortable Environment: Discuss important matters in a private and comfortable environment where both partners feel safe and at ease.

- Distraction-Free: Choose a setting free from distractions to ensure both partners can focus fully on the conversation.

By incorporating these key components into your communication practices, you can build a solid foundation for a healthy, fulfilling relationship. Effective communication fosters mutual understanding, respect, and intimacy, allowing both partners to navigate challenges and celebrate successes together.

4.2 Active Listening Techniques

Active listening is a crucial skill for effective communication. It involves fully engaging with the speaker, understanding their message, and responding thoughtfully. Here are some techniques to enhance your active listening skills:

A. Pay Full Attention

1. Focus on the Speaker:

- Undivided Attention: Make an effort to focus entirely on the speaker and what they are saying. Avoid distractions such as checking your phone, looking around the room, or thinking about your response while they are talking.

- Eye Contact: Maintain appropriate eye contact to show that you are engaged and paying attention. This demonstrates respect and interest in the conversation.

B. Show Interest

1. Body Language:

- Open Posture: Maintain an open and receptive posture. Lean slightly forward, nod occasionally, and use facial expressions that show interest and engagement.

- Nonverbal Cues: Use nonverbal cues like nodding, smiling, and making affirmative sounds (e.g., "Mm-hmm," "I see") to signal that you are listening and interested in what the speaker is saying.

C. Reflect and Paraphrase

1. Summarize Key Points:

- Restate: Restate the main points to ensure you have understood correctly. For example, "So what you're saying is..." or "If I understand you correctly, you're feeling..."

- Clarification: This not only shows that you are listening but also helps clarify any misunderstandings early in the conversation.

D. Ask Open-Ended Questions

1. Encouraging Elaboration:

- Inviting Discussion: Ask questions that encourage the speaker to elaborate on their points. Questions like "Can you tell me more about that?" or "How did that make you feel?" invite deeper discussion and provide more insight into their thoughts and feelings.

- Exploration: Use open-ended questions to explore the topic further and understand the speaker's perspective in greater depth.

E. Avoid Interrupting

1. Patient Listening:

- Wait Your Turn: Wait for your turn to speak and fully absorb what the speaker is saying. Interrupting can disrupt the speaker's train of thought and prevent you from fully understanding their message.

- Respectful Silence: Allow for pauses and silence in the conversation. This gives the speaker time to think and encourages more thoughtful communication.

F. Respond Thoughtfully

1. Thoughtful Replies:

- Considered Responses: Craft responses that show you have carefully considered the speaker's message. Reflect on what they have said before replying, and avoid giving knee-jerk reactions.

- Empathetic Responses: Show empathy in your responses by acknowledging the speaker's feelings and perspectives. Use phrases like, "I understand why you feel that way" or "It sounds like that was really challenging for you."

By incorporating these active listening techniques, you can enhance your communication skills, foster deeper understanding, and build stronger connections with your partner. Active listening demonstrates respect, empathy, and genuine interest, which are essential components of a healthy and fulfilling relationship.

4.3 Nonverbal Communication Cues

Nonverbal communication plays a significant role in conveying emotions and intentions. Understanding and effectively using nonverbal cues can enhance your communication skills. Here are key aspects to consider:

A. Body Language

1. Posture:

- Openness: Stand or sit in a way that shows you are open to communication. Avoid crossing your arms or legs, which can appear defensive or closed off.

- Engagement: Lean slightly forward to show interest and engagement in the conversation. Maintain a relaxed but attentive posture.

2. Gestures:

- Complementary Gestures: Use hand gestures to complement your verbal communication. Be mindful not to overuse them, which can be distracting.

B. Facial Expressions

1. Expressive Faces:

- Convey Emotions: Use your facial expressions to convey empathy, understanding, and other emotions. A smile can show friendliness, while a concerned look can show empathy.

- Match Emotions: Ensure your facial expressions match the emotions you are trying to convey in your verbal communication.

2. Responsiveness:

- Reactive Expressions: React to what the other person is saying with appropriate facial expressions. Nod in agreement or raise your eyebrows in surprise to show you are engaged.

C. Eye Contact

1. Balanced Eye Contact:

- Engagement: Maintain eye contact to show that you are focused and engaged in the conversation. Eye contact can convey interest, attention, and sincerity.

- Comfort: Avoid staring, which can make others uncomfortable. Aim for natural breaks in eye contact to keep the interaction comfortable.

2. Cultural Sensitivity:

- Cultural Norms: Be aware of cultural differences regarding eye contact. In some cultures, prolonged eye contact can be considered disrespectful or confrontational.

D. Tone of Voice

1. Vocal Variety:

- Emotion Expression: Use your voice to express different emotions and keep the conversation engaging. Vary your pitch, volume, and pace to match the emotional tone of the conversation.

- Clarity: Speak clearly and at an appropriate volume to ensure your message is understood. Avoid monotone delivery, which can be perceived as uninterested or disengaged.

2. Emphasis:

- Highlight Points: Use changes in tone to emphasize important points and convey enthusiasm or concern.

E. Personal Space

1. Appropriate Distance:

- Proximity Awareness: Gauge how close to stand or sit based on your relationship with the person and the context of the conversation. Respect personal space to avoid making the other person feel uncomfortable.

- Adjustment: Adjust your distance according to the other person's body language cues. If they lean back or step away, give them more space.

2. Situational Context:

- Context Sensitivity: In intimate conversations, closer proximity may be appropriate, while in professional or casual interactions, a greater distance is usually preferred.

F. Touch

1. Respect Boundaries:

- Appropriate Touch: Ensure any physical touch is welcome and appropriate for the situation. A light touch on the arm can be comforting, but always be mindful of the other person's comfort level.

- Consent: Pay attention to the other person's reactions to touch and seek consent when necessary. If unsure, it's better to err on the side of caution.

2. Contextual Touch:

- Situational Appropriateness: In professional settings, touch should be minimal and appropriate (e.g., a handshake). In personal relationships, more frequent and varied touch can be appropriate if both parties are comfortable.

By understanding and effectively using nonverbal communication cues, you can enhance your interactions and build stronger connections with others. Nonverbal communication often conveys more than words alone, making it a crucial aspect of effective communication.

4.4 Navigating Difficult Conversations

Difficult conversations are inevitable in any relationship. Handling them effectively can prevent misunderstandings and strengthen your bond. Here are strategies for navigating challenging discussions:

A. Prepare Mentally and Emotionally

1. Mental Preparation:

- Clarity of Thought: Think through what you want to say and how you want to say it. Outline your main points and anticipate possible responses.

- Emotion Management: Recognize your own emotions and ensure you are in a calm state of mind before initiating the conversation. This helps you stay focused and clear-headed.

2. Emotional Readiness:

- Self-Reflection: Reflect on your feelings and motivations for having the conversation. Understand why the issue is important to you and what you hope to achieve.

- Positive Mindset: Approach the conversation with a positive mindset, aiming for resolution and understanding rather than conflict.

B. Choose the Right Time and Place

1. Privacy and Comfort:

- Private Setting: Find a setting where both parties feel safe and comfortable, free from distractions and interruptions. This could be at home, in a quiet room, or a neutral place where you both feel at ease.

- Timing: Choose a time when both parties are not rushed, stressed, or preoccupied. Ensure that you both have enough time to discuss the issue thoroughly.

2. Context Consideration:

- Appropriate Moment: Avoid bringing up difficult topics during high-stress situations or when either party is tired or emotionally charged.

C. Stay Calm and Composed

1. Calm Demeanor:

- Emotional Regulation: Keep your emotions in check to help the conversation stay productive. Take deep breaths, pause if needed, and maintain a steady tone.

- Non-Verbal Cues: Ensure your body language conveys calmness and openness. Avoid crossing your arms, raising your voice, or making aggressive gestures.

2. Emotional Control:

- Pause and Reflect: If you feel emotions rising, take a moment to pause and reflect before responding. This helps prevent reactive and unproductive responses.

D. Use "I" Statements

1. Non-Accusatory Language:

- Personal Perspective: Focus on your feelings and experiences rather than blaming the other person. Use "I" statements such as "I feel..." or "I noticed..." instead of "You always..." or "You never..."

- Ownership: Take ownership of your emotions and reactions, which can reduce defensiveness and open up a more constructive dialogue.

2. Specificity:

- Clear Communication: Be specific about your feelings and the behavior that triggered them. For example, "I feel hurt when plans change at the last minute without notice."

E. Listen Actively and Empathetically

1. Empathetic Listening:

- Understanding: Understand and acknowledge the other person's feelings. Show empathy by saying things like, "I understand that you feel upset because..."

- Validation: Validate their emotions even if you don't agree with their perspective. This demonstrates respect and a willingness to see their side.

2. Active Engagement:

- Full Attention: Give your full attention to the speaker, making eye contact, and nodding to show you are listening.

- Reflect and Paraphrase: Reflect back what the other person is saying to ensure understanding. For example, "It sounds like you're feeling... because..."

F. Seek to Understand, Not Win

1. Mutual Understanding:

- Collaborative Approach: Aim for solutions that respect both parties' perspectives. The goal is to understand each other better, not to win an argument.

- Open-Mindedness: Be open to their viewpoint and willing to compromise. This fosters a collaborative rather than adversarial atmosphere.

2. Common Ground:

- Shared Goals: Focus on shared goals and mutual interests to find common ground and work towards a resolution that benefits both parties.

G. Stay Focused on the Issue

1. Issue-Specific Discussion:

- Current Problem: Stick to the current problem to avoid complicating the conversation. Bringing up past issues or unrelated topics can derail the discussion and create more conflict.

- Clarity: Clearly define the issue at hand and keep the conversation centered on finding a resolution for that specific problem.

2. Avoid Generalizations:

- Specific Examples: Use specific examples rather than making generalizations. This helps keep the conversation grounded in reality and prevents misunderstandings.

H. Agree on Action Steps

1. Clear Resolutions:

- Next Steps: Make sure both parties know what steps will be taken next. Clearly outline any actions that need to be taken to resolve the issue.

- Commitment: Ensure that both parties are committed to the agreed-upon action steps. This helps in maintaining accountability and moving forward constructively.

2. Follow-Up:

- Review Progress: Plan a follow-up discussion to review progress and make any necessary adjustments. This ensures that both parties are on track and that the resolution is working.

Chapter 4 Review: Basics of Effective Communication

Effective communication is fundamental to building and maintaining healthy relationships. This chapter explores the essential elements of effective communication, including clarity, honesty, respect, and empathy. It also covers crucial skills such as active listening, understanding nonverbal cues, and navigating difficult conversations.

4.1 The Foundations of Communication

- Clarity and Conciseness: Speak clearly and directly, using simple language to avoid misunderstandings.

- Honesty and Openness: Be truthful and open about your thoughts and feelings to build trust.

- Respect and Empathy: Communicate with respect and empathy, acknowledging your partner's feelings.

- Feedback and Reflection: Provide constructive feedback and reflect on your own communication patterns to improve.

- Timing and Context: Choose the right time and place for important conversations to ensure both parties are calm and available to talk.

4.2 Active Listening Techniques

- Pay Full Attention: Focus entirely on the speaker, avoiding distractions.

- Show Interest: Use verbal and nonverbal cues to show you are listening.

- Reflect and Paraphrase: Repeat what the speaker has said in your own words to ensure understanding.

- Ask Open-Ended Questions: Encourage the speaker to elaborate with questions that require more than yes or no answers.

- Avoid Interrupting: Let the speaker finish their thoughts without interruption.

- Respond Thoughtfully: Consider your response before speaking to ensure it is thoughtful and considerate.

4.3 Nonverbal Communication Cues

- Body Language: Use open body language to indicate receptivity and openness.

- Facial Expressions: Reflect your emotions through facial expressions to enhance your verbal message.

- Eye Contact: Maintain eye contact to show interest and confidence.

- Tone of Voice: Use a warm and calm tone to convey empathy and avoid harsh tones.

- Personal Space: Respect personal space to ensure comfort.

- Touch: Use appropriate physical touch to convey support and affection, respecting personal boundaries.

4.4 Navigating Difficult Conversations

- Prepare Mentally and Emotionally: Think through your points and anticipate reactions.

- Choose the Right Time and Place: Ensure a private and comfortable setting for the conversation.

- Stay Calm and Composed: Maintain a calm demeanor and take deep breaths if needed.

- Use "I" Statements: Express feelings and concerns using "I" statements to avoid sounding accusatory.

- Listen Actively and Empathetically: Understand and acknowledge your partner's feelings without interrupting.

- Seek to Understand, Not Win: Aim for mutual understanding and compromise.

- Stay Focused on the Issue: Keep the conversation focused on the specific issue at hand.

- Agree on Action Steps: Conclude by agreeing on actionable steps to address the issue.

Summary

Mastering the basics of effective communication is essential for building and maintaining healthy relationships. By understanding the foundations of communication, practicing active listening, utilizing nonverbal cues, and navigating difficult conversations with skill, you can enhance your interactions and deepen your connections with others. This chapter provides practical tools and techniques to help you communicate more effectively and create a stronger, more supportive relationship.

Chapter 5: Enhancing Communication in Relationships

Effective communication is crucial for nurturing and sustaining healthy relationships. This chapter explores advanced communication techniques to help you express yourself clearly, navigate digital communication, resolve conflicts, and practice apologizing and forgiving. By mastering these skills, you can foster deeper connections and enhance the overall quality of your relationships.

5.1 Expressing Yourself Clearly

Clear communication involves articulating your thoughts, feelings, and needs in a way that your partner can easily understand. Here's how to express yourself clearly:

A. Be Direct and Specific

1. Use Concrete Examples:

- Illustrate Points: Provide specific instances to illustrate your points, making your communication more impactful and understandable. For example, instead of saying "You never help around the house," say "I felt overwhelmed last week when I had to do all the house chores alone."

2. Avoid Generalizations:

- Precision: Refrain from using words like "always" or "never," as they can lead to defensiveness. These words can exaggerate the issue and distract from the main point.

B. Use "I" Statements

1. Own Your Feelings:

- Responsibility: Take responsibility for your emotions rather than blaming your partner for how you feel. Use "I" statements such as "I feel upset when..." instead of "You make me feel...".

2. Avoid Blame:

- Focus on Impact: Focus on how the situation affects you rather than what your partner did wrong. This approach reduces defensiveness and opens up a more constructive dialogue.

C. Stay on Topic

1. Focus on Solutions:

- Future-Oriented: Discuss what can be done to improve the situation rather than dwelling on past mistakes. This keeps the conversation productive and forward-looking.

2. Avoid Bringing Up the Past:

- Present Issue: Stick to the current issue to keep the conversation productive. Bringing up past grievances can complicate the discussion and lead to unresolved conflicts resurfacing.

D. Be Honest and Authentic

1. Vulnerability:

- True Self: Be willing to be vulnerable and share your true self. This openness can strengthen your emotional connection and build trust.

2. Trust:

- Empathy: Trust that your partner will respond with empathy and support. Honesty fosters a deeper understanding and mutual respect in the relationship.

E. Check for Understanding

1. Clarification:

- Encourage Questions: Encourage your partner to ask questions if they are unsure about what you said. This helps to clear up any misunderstandings immediately.

2. Feedback Loop:

- Confirm Understanding: Use feedback to confirm mutual understanding. Paraphrase what your partner says and ask them to do the same to ensure both parties are on the same page.

F. Practice Active Listening

1. Full Attention:

- Undivided Attention: Give your partner your undivided attention during conversations. Put away distractions like phones or other devices to show that you are fully present.

2. Nonverbal Cues:

- Body Language: Use body language to show that you are actively listening. Maintain eye contact, nod in agreement, and lean slightly forward to show engagement.

By following these strategies, you can express yourself more clearly and effectively. Clear communication helps prevent misunderstandings, resolves conflicts, and strengthens your bond with your partner. This approach fosters a healthy and supportive relationship where both parties feel heard, valued, and understood.

5.2 Digital Communication Etiquette

In today's digital age, much of our communication happens online. Understanding digital communication etiquette can help maintain healthy relationships:

A. Be Mindful of Tone

1. Tone Indicators:

- Convey Emotion: Use emojis or punctuation to convey tone and emotion. For example, a smiley face can indicate friendliness, while an exclamation mark can show excitement.

- Clarify Intent: Be clear and precise to prevent misunderstandings. Text lacks the nuance of voice, so indicating tone helps ensure your message is received as intended.

2. Avoid Misinterpretation:

- Explicit Language: Choose your words carefully to avoid ambiguity. If a message could be interpreted in multiple ways, rephrase it for clarity.

- Contextual Cues: Provide context when necessary to help the recipient understand your message better.

B. Respond Promptly

1. Timeliness:

- Show Value: Respond within a reasonable time frame to show you value the communication. Prompt responses demonstrate respect and attentiveness.

- Acknowledge Receipt: If you can't provide a full response immediately, acknowledge the message and indicate when you will reply.

2. Prioritize Important Messages:

- Urgency: Address urgent or important messages promptly. Prioritize communications that require immediate attention to avoid misunderstandings or missed opportunities.

C. Use Emojis and Punctuation

1. Enhance Clarity:

- Readable Messages: Use punctuation to make your messages clear and easy to read. Proper punctuation helps avoid confusion and ensures your message is understood.

- Structured Text: Break up long messages into paragraphs or bullet points to improve readability.

2. Express Emotions:

- Emoji Use: Emojis can help convey your feelings more accurately. They add a personal touch and make your messages more relatable.

- Balance: Use emojis appropriately and sparingly to complement your text, not overshadow it.

D. Avoid Sensitive Topics via Text

1. Choose the Right Medium:

- Simple Communication: Use text for simple, straightforward communication. For complex or emotional discussions, opt for face-to-face or voice calls.

- Sensitive Issues: Discuss sensitive topics in person or over a call to ensure nuances are communicated and both parties can fully express themselves.

2. Context Matters:

- Appropriate Medium: Ensure the communication method fits the message. Consider the gravity of the topic and choose the medium that best supports a meaningful conversation.

E. Respect Privacy

1. Confidentiality:

- Trust Building: Keep private messages confidential to build trust. Avoid sharing personal messages or details with others without consent.

- Discretion: Handle sensitive information with care, respecting your partner's privacy.

2. Boundaries:

- Comfort Level: Respect your partner's comfort level with digital sharing. Understand their preferences for public and private communication.

F. Limit Over-Communication

1. Healthy Balance:

- Mutual Rhythm: Find a communication rhythm that works for both partners. Too much communication can feel overwhelming, while too little can create distance.

- Quality over Quantity: Focus on meaningful exchanges rather than constant updates.

2. Space and Independence:

- Recharge Time: Allow each other time and space to recharge. Respecting personal space helps maintain a healthy balance in the relationship.

- Independence: Encourage independence by not expecting immediate responses at all times.

By following these digital communication etiquette guidelines, you can maintain clear, respectful, and effective communication with your partner. This approach fosters a healthy digital relationship, where both parties feel valued, understood, and respected.

5.3 Conflict Resolution Strategies

Conflicts are a natural part of any relationship. Handling them effectively can strengthen your bond and improve understanding. Here are some conflict resolution strategies:

A. Stay Calm and Composed

1. Emotional Regulation:

- Deep Breathing: Practice techniques to stay calm, such as deep breathing, counting to ten, or mindfulness exercises. These techniques help regulate your emotions and prevent impulsive reactions.

- Pause and Reflect: Take a moment to pause and reflect before responding. This helps you approach the situation with a clear mind and controlled emotions.

2. Avoid Escalation:

- Calm Demeanor: Keep your emotions in check to prevent the conflict from escalating. Avoid raising your voice, using aggressive body language, or making hostile comments.

- Non-Reactive: Respond to inflammatory remarks with calmness and composure to de-escalate the situation.

B. Focus on the Issue, Not the Person

1. Separate Person from Problem:

- Issue-Centric: Focus on the issue at hand rather than personal attacks. Avoid blaming or criticizing your partner's character.

- Objective Perspective: Discuss the specific behavior or situation that is causing the conflict, not the individual.

2. Constructive Criticism:

- Behavioral Feedback: Provide feedback that addresses behaviors, not character. Use statements like, "I feel upset when you..." instead of "You are always..."

- Positive Framing: Frame your feedback in a way that encourages positive change rather than inducing defensiveness.

C. Listen Actively

1. Empathetic Listening:

- Show Understanding: Show that you understand and respect their viewpoint. Use verbal affirmations and nodding to convey empathy.

- Emotional Validation: Acknowledge their feelings, even if you don't agree with their perspective. This demonstrates respect for their emotions.

2. Reflective Listening:

- Paraphrase: Paraphrase what they've said to ensure understanding. For example, "So, you're feeling frustrated because..."

- Clarify: Ask clarifying questions if you're unsure about their point. This helps avoid misunderstandings and ensures both parties are on the same page.

D. Seek Common Ground

1. Shared Goals:

- Common Objectives: Focus on shared objectives to foster cooperation. Identify common interests and goals that both partners want to achieve.

- Unity: Emphasize that you are a team working towards a common solution.

2. Compromise:

- Middle Ground: Be willing to find a middle ground that satisfies both partners. Flexibility and willingness to give and take are key to resolving conflicts.

- Balanced Solutions: Ensure that the compromise addresses the needs and concerns of both parties fairly.

E. Use Problem-Solving Techniques

1. Collaborative Solutions:

- Joint Effort: Work together to find solutions that address both partners' needs. Approach the problem as a team rather than adversaries.

- Brainstorming: Generate multiple solutions and discuss the pros and cons of each option.

2. Pros and Cons:

- Evaluate Options: Evaluate potential solutions to find the best approach. Consider the benefits and drawbacks of each solution and choose the one that works best for both parties.

F. Take Breaks if Needed

1. Cooling Off:

- Pause: Use breaks to prevent saying things you might regret. If emotions are running high, take a short break to cool off and collect your thoughts.

- Temporary Separation: Agree on a temporary separation if needed to prevent further escalation.

2. Scheduled Return:

- Agree on Time: Agree on a time to continue the discussion after the break. This ensures that the conversation will resume in a more composed and thoughtful manner.

- Commitment: Commit to returning to the discussion and resolving the issue.

G. Agree to Disagree

1. Respect Differences:

- Acceptance: Accept that not all disagreements can be resolved. Some issues may require agreeing to disagree while maintaining respect for each other's perspectives.

- Diverse Views: Recognize that differing opinions are natural and can coexist within a healthy relationship.

2. Focus on Harmony:

- Respect and Harmony: Maintain respect and harmony despite differing opinions. Focus on what you appreciate about each other and the relationship as a whole.

- Relationship Priorities: Prioritize the health and happiness of the relationship over winning the argument.

By implementing these conflict resolution strategies, you can navigate disagreements more effectively and foster a stronger, more understanding relationship. Handling conflicts with calmness, empathy, and a focus on solutions will strengthen your bond and enhance mutual respect.

5.4 Apologizing and Forgiving

Apologizing and forgiving are essential for healing and maintaining trust in relationships. Here's how to practice these important skills:

A. Offer a Sincere Apology

1. Full Accountability:

- Responsibility: Take full responsibility for your actions without making excuses or shifting blame. Acknowledge what you did wrong and accept the consequences.

- Ownership: Use statements like "I was wrong for..." or "I apologize for..." to show that you recognize your fault.

2. Avoid Defensiveness:

- Open Acknowledgment: Acknowledge your mistakes without defending them. Avoid justifying your behavior or explaining why you did it in a way that diminishes the apology.

B. Explain the Impact

1. Acknowledge Harm:

- Validation: Recognize and validate the impact of your actions on your partner. Show that you understand how your behavior affected them.

- Impact Statements: Use statements like "I realize that my actions hurt you because..." to convey your understanding of the harm caused.

2. Empathy:

- Emotional Understanding: Show empathy for your partner's feelings. Express that you are genuinely sorry for the pain or inconvenience you caused.

- Compassion: Demonstrate compassion by acknowledging their emotions and offering support.

C. Commit to Change

1. Action Plan:

- Prevent Recurrence: Develop a plan to prevent the issue from recurring. Outline specific steps you will take to change your behavior.

- Proactive Measures: Share your action plan with your partner to show your commitment to improvement.

2. Consistency:

- Follow-Through: Consistently demonstrate your commitment to change through your actions. Regularly review and adjust your plan as needed.

- Long-Term Effort: Show that your commitment to change is not just temporary but a sustained effort.

D. Allow Time for Healing

1. Patience:

- Emotional Space: Allow your partner the time they need to heal. Respect their need for space and time to process their emotions.

- Non-Pressuring: Avoid pressuring your partner to forgive or move on quickly.

2. Supportive Presence:

- Availability: Be there for your partner as they process their emotions. Offer support without being overbearing.

- Understanding: Show understanding and patience as they work through their feelings.

E. Practice Self-Forgiveness

1. Self-Compassion:

- Kindness to Self: Treat yourself with the same compassion you would offer to others. Recognize that making mistakes is a part of being human.

- Positive Affirmations: Use positive affirmations to rebuild your self-esteem and confidence.

2. Learn and Grow:

- Growth Opportunities: Use mistakes as opportunities for growth and self-improvement. Reflect on what you can learn from the situation.

- Continuous Improvement: Commit to continuous personal development and betterment.

F. Seek Forgiveness Gracefully

1. Open-Hearted Forgiveness:

- Genuine Desire: Be willing to forgive and move forward. Show that you genuinely want to heal the relationship.

- Reconciliation Efforts: Make sincere efforts to reconcile and rebuild trust.

2. Release Resentment:

- Letting Go: Let go of grudges to maintain relationship health. Holding onto resentment can prevent healing and hinder the relationship.

- Emotional Freedom: Embrace emotional freedom by releasing past hurts and focusing on positive aspects of the relationship.

G. Discuss Forgiveness Openly

1. Mutual Understanding:

- Open Dialogue: Ensure both partners are on the same page regarding forgiveness. Discuss what forgiveness means to each of you and how you can achieve it.

- Expectation Setting: Set clear expectations about what forgiveness entails and how you will move forward together.

2. Clear Path Forward:

- Action Steps: Define steps for moving forward together. Create a shared vision for your relationship's future.

- Collaborative Efforts: Work together to rebuild trust and strengthen your bond.

Chapter 5 Review: Enhancing Communication in Relationships

Effective communication is vital for nurturing and sustaining healthy relationships. This chapter explores advanced communication techniques to help you express yourself clearly, navigate digital communication, resolve conflicts, and practice apologizing and forgiving.

5.1 Expressing Yourself Clearly

- Be Direct and Specific: Clearly state what you want or need, using concrete examples to avoid misunderstandings.

- Use "I" Statements: Focus on your feelings and needs without blaming your partner.

- Stay on Topic: Keep conversations focused on the current issue without bringing up past grievances.

- Be Honest and Authentic: Share your true thoughts and feelings to build trust.

- Check for Understanding: Ensure your partner understands your message through clarification and feedback.

- Practice Active Listening: Show engagement and interest by listening without interrupting and responding thoughtfully.

5.2 Digital Communication Etiquette

- Be Mindful of Tone: Use clear language and consider how your words might be received to avoid misinterpretation.

- Respond Promptly: Address messages in a timely manner to show you value the communication.

- Use Emojis and Punctuation: Enhance clarity and convey emotions accurately in your messages.

- Avoid Sensitive Topics via Text: Discuss important matters in person or through video calls to ensure nuanced communication.

- Respect Privacy: Keep private conversations confidential and respect digital boundaries.

- Limit Over-Communication: Balance message frequency to avoid overwhelming your partner and respect their need for space.

5.3 Conflict Resolution Strategies

- Stay Calm and Composed: Manage your emotions before engaging in a discussion to prevent escalation.

- Focus on the Issue, Not the Person: Address the specific issue constructively without attacking your partner.

- Listen Actively: Give your partner the opportunity to express their perspective and show empathy.

- Seek Common Ground: Identify areas of agreement and build on them to find mutually acceptable solutions.

- Use Problem-Solving Techniques: Approach conflicts collaboratively to develop effective solutions.

- Take Breaks if Needed: If conflicts become too heated, agree on a time to revisit the conversation when calmer.

- Agree to Disagree: Respect each other's viewpoints and find ways to move forward despite differences.

5.4 Apologizing and Forgiving

- Offer a Sincere Apology: Acknowledge your mistake, express remorse, and take responsibility without making excuses.

- Explain the Impact: Show that you understand the consequences of your behavior on your partner.

- Commit to Change: Promise to make amends and avoid repeating the mistake, and follow through consistently.

- Allow Time for Healing: Be patient and give your partner space to process their feelings.

- Practice Self-Forgiveness: Forgive yourself for past mistakes and use them as opportunities for growth.

- Seek Forgiveness Gracefully: Be open to forgiving when on the receiving end of an apology, and let go of grudges.

- Discuss Forgiveness Openly: Have clear discussions about forgiveness and how to move forward together.

Summary

Enhancing communication in relationships involves expressing yourself clearly, practicing digital communication etiquette, employing effective conflict resolution strategies, and mastering the art of apologizing and forgiving. These skills foster deeper understanding, trust, and intimacy, contributing to the long-term success and fulfillment of your relationships.

Part 3: Finding a Partner

Chapter 6: Modern Dating Landscape

Navigating the modern dating landscape involves a blend of online and traditional methods, effectively using social media, and balancing dating with personal life. By choosing the right dating platforms, engaging in traditional social activities, managing your social media presence, and maintaining a healthy balance between dating and personal life, you can enhance your chances of finding a meaningful and fulfilling relationship. This chapter provides practical tools and strategies to help you successfully navigate the complexities of modern dating and build a strong foundation for lasting connections.

6.1 Online Dating and Apps

Online dating and apps have revolutionized the way people meet and connect. Here's a comprehensive guide to navigating this modern dating landscape:

A. Choosing the Right Platform

1. Examples of Apps:

- Tinder: Known for casual dating and a large user base. Ideal for those looking for a variety of dating experiences.

- Bumble: Women-initiated contact; empowering women to make the first move. Suitable for those who prefer a more balanced approach to initiating conversations.

- Hinge: Relationship-focused with prompts to encourage meaningful conversations. Good for those seeking long-term relationships.

- Niche Apps: Platforms like FarmersOnly (for rural dating) or JDate (for Jewish singles) cater to specific interests and communities, making it easier to find like-minded individuals.

2. Read Reviews and Testimonials:

- User Feedback: Look at user reviews and success stories to determine which app might suit your preferences. Consider factors like user demographics, app features, and overall user satisfaction.

- Platform Reputation: Research the app's reputation regarding safety, privacy, and success rates.

B. Creating an Engaging Profile

1. Photo Tips:

- Variety: Use a mix of solo photos and those showing you engaged in activities you enjoy. This gives potential matches a well-rounded view of your personality and interests.

- Quality: Ensure your photos are clear, recent, and well-lit. Avoid group photos that can make it hard to identify you.

2. Bio Tips:

- Honesty: Be honest and specific about your interests and what you seek in a relationship. Authenticity attracts like-minded individuals and sets the right expectations.

- Engaging Content: Use humor, anecdotes, or unique facts about yourself to make your bio stand out.

C. Safety First

1. Avoid Sharing Personal Details Early:

- Privacy: Keep your full name, address, and workplace private initially. Use the app's messaging system until you feel comfortable sharing more personal information.

- Secure Communication: Be cautious with sharing your phone number or social media profiles too soon.

2. Report Suspicious Behavior:

- App Features: Use the app's features to report any suspicious or inappropriate behavior. Most platforms have mechanisms in place to address safety concerns.

- Trust Your Instincts: If something feels off, don't hesitate to block or report the user.

D. Effective Communication

1. Personalized Openers:

- Genuine Interest: Reference something specific from their profile to show genuine interest. This demonstrates that you've taken the time to read their profile and are truly interested.

- Unique Starters: Avoid generic openers and instead ask questions or comment on shared interests.

2. Maintain Respectful Communication:

- Politeness: Be polite and respectful in all interactions. Kindness and respect set a positive tone for the conversation.

- Boundaries: Respect personal boundaries and avoid pushing for personal details or commitments too soon.

E. Managing Expectations

1. Set Clear Intentions:

- Transparency: Be upfront about whether you're looking for something casual or serious. Clear intentions help both parties understand the nature of the relationship.

- Profile Clarity: Ensure your profile reflects your intentions to attract compatible matches.

2. Be Open to Different Outcomes:

- Flexibility: Understand that dating is a process of discovery and not all matches will be perfect. Stay open to different outcomes and experiences.

- Learning Opportunity: View each date as an opportunity to learn more about yourself and what you're looking for.

F. Setting Up Dates

1. Public Locations:

- Safety First: Opt for coffee shops, parks, or restaurants. Public places ensure safety and provide a comfortable environment for both parties.

- Accessibility: Choose locations that are easy to reach for both parties.

2. First Date Tips:

- Casual Approach: Keep it casual and light. A relaxed setting helps reduce pressure and allows for natural conversation.

- Exit Plan: Have an exit plan if things don't go well. This could be a pre-planned activity or a friend checking in on you.

Navigating online dating and apps effectively requires choosing the right platform, creating an engaging profile, prioritizing safety, communicating effectively, managing expectations, and setting up dates thoughtfully. By following these guidelines, you can enhance your online dating experience, increase your chances of finding meaningful connections, and ensure that your dating journey is enjoyable and safe.

6.2 Traditional Dating Methods

While online dating is popular, traditional methods of meeting people are still effective and often lead to meaningful connections. Here are some traditional dating methods to consider:

A. Social Events and Gatherings

1. Be Open and Approachable:

- Positive Body Language: Smile, make eye contact, and maintain an open posture. These nonverbal cues invite others to engage with you.

- Initiate Conversations: Be willing to start conversations with new people. Ask open-ended questions and show genuine interest in their responses.

2. *Follow Up:*

- Keep in Touch: If you meet someone interesting, follow up with a message or plan to meet again. Suggest an activity or event you both might enjoy.

- Exchange Contact Information: Don't be shy about exchanging phone numbers or social media handles to stay connected.

B. Hobbies and Interests

1. Regular Participation:

- Consistency: Attend regularly to build familiarity and rapport with other members. Being a regular participant makes you more approachable and recognizable.

- Engage Actively: Participate actively in the activities and engage with others who share your interests.

2. Initiate Activities:

- Group Outings: Suggest group outings or activities to deepen connections. This could be anything from a hiking trip to a movie night.

- Event Planning: Take the initiative to plan or organize events, which can help you stand out and make meaningful connections.

C. Networking Events

1. Prepare Your Introduction:

- Engaging Introduction: Have a concise and engaging way to introduce yourself. Highlight key aspects of who you are and what you do.

- Confidence: Approach people with confidence and a friendly demeanor.

2. Exchange Contact Information:

- Proactive Approach: Be proactive in exchanging business cards or contact details. Follow up with a friendly message to continue the conversation.

- Networking Mindset: Remember that networking events are not just about business; they can also be great opportunities for social connections.

D. Introductions Through Friends and Family

1. Express Interest:

- Open Communication: Let your friends and family know you're open to being introduced to someone. They can be valuable matchmakers.

- Express Preferences: Share your preferences and what you're looking for in a partner, but remain open to their suggestions.

2. Be Open-Minded:

- Fair Chance: Give introductions a fair chance, even if the person doesn't immediately seem like your type. You might be surprised by the connection you develop.

- Positive Attitude: Approach each introduction with a positive attitude and an open heart.

E. Volunteering

1. Choose Causes You Care About:

- Passion-Driven: This ensures genuine interactions with people who share your values and passions. It also makes the experience more enjoyable and fulfilling for you.

- Active Participation: Be active and engaged in the volunteer work, which naturally facilitates connections with others.

2. Network with Volunteers:

- Socialize: Engage with other volunteers during and after events. Attend related events or social gatherings to expand your network.

- Collaborate: Work closely with other volunteers on projects, which can help build strong, meaningful relationships.

6.3 Navigating Social Media in Dating

Social media plays a significant role in modern dating, offering both opportunities and challenges. Here's how to navigate social media effectively in the dating world:

A. Building a Positive Online Presence

1. Consistent Branding:

- Profile Alignment: Ensure your profile pictures and content align with how you wish to be perceived. Consistent and authentic representation can attract like-minded individuals.

- Positive Image: Highlight your interests and values through your posts. Share content that reflects your hobbies, passions, and positive aspects of your life.

2. Engage Positively:

- Avoid Negativity: Steer clear of negative or controversial posts that could be off-putting. Focus on sharing uplifting and inspiring content.

- Positive Interactions: Engage with others in a friendly and respectful manner, contributing positively to online discussions.

B. Using Social Media for Connection

1. Meaningful Engagement:

- Thoughtful Comments: Comment thoughtfully on posts to show genuine interest. Personalized and sincere interactions can foster deeper connections.

- Engage in Conversations: Participate in meaningful conversations rather than just liking posts. This demonstrates a genuine interest in others.

2. Avoid Overdoing It:

- Balance Interactions: Balance your interactions to avoid coming across as too eager or intrusive. Maintain a natural and respectful pace in your online engagement.

- Moderation: Engage regularly but not excessively, allowing the relationship to develop organically.

C. Balancing Privacy and Transparency

1. Adjust Privacy Settings:

- Control Visibility: Control who can see your posts and personal information. Adjust privacy settings to maintain a balance between openness and privacy.

- Selective Sharing: Share personal details selectively, ensuring you maintain a level of privacy until trust is established.

2. Be Cautious:

- Gradual Sharing: Avoid sharing too much too soon. Gradually reveal more about yourself as the relationship progresses.

- Protect Personal Information: Be mindful of the personal information you share to protect your privacy and security.

D. Avoiding Misinterpretations

1. Clarify Ambiguities:

- Contextualize Posts: If a post might be misunderstood, add context or clarification to avoid misinterpretations. Clear communication helps prevent confusion.

- Transparent Communication: Be transparent about your intentions and the context behind your posts.

2. Address Misunderstandings:

- Prompt Resolution: If misinterpretations arise, address them promptly and openly. Clear up any confusion with direct and honest communication.

- Open Dialogue: Encourage an open dialogue to resolve any misunderstandings and reinforce trust.

E. Managing Relationship Status Online

1. Mutual Agreement:

- Joint Decision: Decide together when and how to announce your relationship status. Ensure both partners are comfortable with the timing and manner of the announcement.

- Respect Preferences: Respect your partner's preferences regarding public displays of your relationship status.

2. Respect Boundaries:

- Comfort Level: Respect your partner's comfort level with public displays of affection online. Avoid posting anything that might make them uncomfortable.

- Consent: Always seek your partner's consent before sharing information or photos related to your relationship.

By navigating social media with awareness and intentionality, you can enhance your dating experience, foster genuine connections, and maintain a healthy balance between your online and offline interactions.

6.4 Balancing Dating with Personal Life

Finding the right balance between dating and personal life is crucial for maintaining overall well-being and ensuring a healthy relationship. Here's how to achieve that balance:

A. Prioritizing Self-Care

1. Self-Care Routine:

- Daily Practices: Develop and maintain a routine that includes activities for self-care such as exercise, healthy eating, and sufficient sleep. This ensures you stay healthy and energized.

- Personal Time: Dedicate time for hobbies and interests that bring you joy and relaxation.

2. Stress Management:

- Relaxation Techniques: Use techniques like meditation, yoga, or journaling to manage stress. These practices can help you stay calm and focused.

- Mindfulness: Incorporate mindfulness practices to stay present and reduce anxiety related to dating and personal life.

B. Setting Boundaries

1. Time Management:

- Scheduling: Schedule your dates around your personal and professional responsibilities. This helps maintain a balance and prevents neglecting important areas of your life.

- Planner Use: Utilize a planner or digital calendar to organize your time effectively.

2. Respecting Limits:

- Clear Communication: Communicate your availability and stick to your boundaries. Let your partner know when you need personal time.

- Consistency: Consistently uphold your boundaries to avoid burnout and maintain personal well-being.

C. Communicating Expectations

1. Honesty:

- Realistic Commitments: Be honest about how much time you can realistically devote to dating. This prevents unrealistic expectations and potential conflicts.

- Open Dialogue: Keep an open dialogue with your partner about your availability and commitments.

2. Mutual Understanding:

- Schedule Coordination: Ensure both partners understand and respect each other's schedules and commitments. Work together to find a balance that works for both.

D. Scheduling Quality Time

1. Plan Dates Thoughtfully:

- Meaningful Activities: Schedule dates that are meaningful and enjoyable. Choose activities that both partners find fulfilling.

- Variety: Incorporate a variety of date ideas to keep things interesting and engaging.

2. Personal Time:

- Balance: Make sure to have time for your own hobbies and relaxation. Balance time spent together with personal downtime.

- Solo Activities: Encourage each other to pursue individual interests and activities.

E. Reflecting on Your Priorities

1. Periodic Review:

- Self-Assessment: Assess whether your dating activities align with your personal goals and values. Reflect on how dating fits into your overall life plan.

- Balance Check: Regularly check if you're maintaining a healthy balance between dating and other aspects of your life.

2. Adjustments:

- Flexible Approach: Be willing to make changes to maintain balance and well-being. Adjust your dating schedule as needed to prioritize self-care and personal responsibilities.

- Reevaluation: Continuously reevaluate your priorities and make necessary adjustments.

F. Evaluating Relationships

1. Regular Check-Ins:

- Open Discussions: Discuss with your partner how the relationship is going. Regular check-ins help ensure both partners are satisfied and on the same page.

- Feedback: Provide and receive feedback constructively to improve the relationship.

2. Value Assessment:

- Positive Contribution: Determine if the relationship positively contributes to your life. Reflect on whether it enhances your well-being and supports your personal goals.

- Growth and Support: Assess if the relationship encourages personal growth and provides mutual support.

By effectively balancing dating with personal life, you can maintain your overall well-being and build a healthier, more fulfilling relationship.

Prioritizing self-care, setting boundaries, communicating expectations, scheduling quality time, reflecting on your priorities, and evaluating your relationships are all crucial steps in achieving this balance.

Chapter 6 Review: Modern Dating Landscape

Navigating the modern dating landscape requires a blend of online and traditional methods, effective use of social media, and maintaining a balance between dating and personal life.

6.1 Online Dating and Apps

- Choosing the Right Platform: Select a dating app that aligns with your goals, whether for casual dating, serious relationships, or niche interests.

- Creating an Engaging Profile: Use high-quality photos and write an honest, specific bio to attract compatible matches.

- Safety First: Protect personal information and use the app's messaging system until comfortable moving to other communication methods.

- Effective Communication: Start conversations with thoughtful, personalized messages and maintain respectful communication.

- Managing Expectations: Be realistic about outcomes and set clear intentions for what you seek.

- Setting Up Dates: Arrange first dates in public places and keep them simple and low-pressure.

6.2 Traditional Dating Methods

- Social Events and Gatherings: Attend parties and gatherings to meet new people in a relaxed environment.

- Hobbies and Interests: Join clubs or groups related to your interests for natural, shared connections.

- Networking Events: Meet potential partners through professional networking opportunities.

- Introductions Through Friends and Family: Leverage your social network for introductions to compatible partners.

- Volunteering: Participate in volunteer activities to meet like-minded individuals.

6.3 Navigating Social Media in Dating

- Building a Positive Online Presence: Ensure your social media profiles reflect your personality and values positively.

- Using Social Media for Connection: Engage with potential partners' posts to start casual conversations and show interest.

- Balancing Privacy and Transparency: Share appropriately and maintain privacy, especially in early dating stages.

- Avoiding Misinterpretations: Be clear in your posts and address any misunderstandings promptly.

- Managing Relationship Status Online: Discuss with your partner how to handle your relationship status on social media.

6.4 Balancing Dating with Personal Life

- Prioritizing Self-Care: Balance dating with activities that nurture your well-being, such as exercise and hobbies.

- Setting Boundaries: Establish clear boundaries for dating time to avoid interfering with personal responsibilities.

- Communicating Expectations: Be open about your availability and commitments with your partner.

- Scheduling Quality Time: Make intentional time for your partner while ensuring time for yourself and other aspects of your life.

- Reflecting on Your Priorities: Regularly assess and adjust your dating approach to align with your goals and values.

- Evaluating Relationships: Periodically evaluate relationships to ensure they are positively contributing to your life.

Summary

This chapter provides practical strategies for successfully navigating the modern dating landscape. By blending online and traditional methods, managing social media presence, and balancing dating with personal life, you can enhance your chances of finding meaningful and fulfilling relationships.

Chapter 7: Creating an Attractive Profile

Your online dating profile is your first impression in the digital dating world. A well-crafted profile can attract the right matches and set the stage for meaningful connections. This chapter guides you through creating an engaging, authentic, and safe profile that showcases your best self.

7.1 Crafting a Compelling Bio

Your bio is one of the first things potential matches will see, and it's your chance to make a great first impression. Here's how to craft a compelling bio that stands out:

A. Be Authentic

1. Genuine Representation:

- Truthfulness: Avoid exaggerating or fabricating details about yourself. Authenticity is attractive and sets the foundation for a genuine connection.

- Honesty: Be straightforward about your interests, hobbies, and what you're looking for in a relationship.

2. Personal Touch:

- Anecdotes: Include anecdotes or small stories to give a real sense of who you are. For example, "I once traveled to Italy just for the pizza – and it was worth every bite!"

B. Showcase Your Personality

1. Conversational Tone:

- Engagement: Write as if you're speaking to someone directly. This makes your bio more relatable and engaging.

- Natural Flow: Use a tone that reflects your natural way of speaking to help potential matches get a feel for your personality.

2. Humor and Quirks:

- Light-heartedness: Share light-hearted, fun aspects of your personality. For instance, "I'm a big fan of dad jokes – the cheesier, the better!"

- Unique Traits: Highlight unique quirks or interests that set you apart from others.

C. Keep It Concise

1. Brevity and Impact:

- Focused Writing: Focus on making every word count. Avoid long-winded descriptions and keep your bio to a few well-crafted sentences.

- Key Highlights: Include the most relevant and interesting information about yourself.

2. Essential Details:

- Priority Information: Prioritize the most important details about yourself, such as your passions, interests, and what you're looking for in a partner.

D. Include a Call to Action

1. Engage Directly:

- Interactive Invite: Invite potential matches to interact with specific interests or activities. For example, "If you love hiking as much as I do, let's find a trail together!"

- Conversation Starters: Provide easy prompts for starting a conversation.

2. Clear Invitation:

- Encouragement: Make it easy for them to start a conversation. For example, "Tell me about your favorite book – I'm always looking for new recommendations!"

E. Be Positive

1. Optimistic Outlook:

- Passions: Highlight your passions and what excites you. Share what makes you happy and what you're enthusiastic about.

- Positive Vibes: Keep the tone of your bio upbeat and welcoming.

2. Avoid Negativity:

- Positive Framing: Avoid mentioning what you don't like or negative experiences. Focus on the positive aspects of your life and what you're looking forward to.

F. Proofread

1. Attention to Detail:

- Typos: Double-check for any typos or errors. A well-written bio reflects attention to detail and care.

- Grammar: Ensure your grammar is correct to maintain professionalism.

2. Professionalism:

- Polished Presentation: A well-crafted and error-free bio shows that you care about making a good impression. It indicates that you put thought and effort into your profile.

By following these tips, you can craft a bio that captures your true self, engages potential matches, and sets the stage for meaningful connections.

7.2 Choosing the Right Photos

Photos are a crucial part of your profile and significantly impact your chances of making connections. Here's how to choose the right photos:

A. Use High-Quality Images

1. Professional Appearance:

- Clarity: Clear, high-quality photos create a better impression. Avoid blurry or pixelated images.

- Presentation: Consider using a good camera or smartphone to ensure your photos are sharp and well-defined.

2. Good Lighting:

- Natural Light: Natural light often works best to enhance your appearance. Take photos in well-lit environments, preferably outdoors or near a window.

- Lighting Techniques: If indoors, ensure the lighting is even and avoid harsh shadows.

B. Show Your Face

1. Face Visibility:

- Clear View: Make sure your face is clearly visible and well-lit. Avoid photos with sunglasses or hats that obscure your face.

- Close-Up Shots: Include a few close-up shots that highlight your facial features.

2. Approachable Expression:

- Friendly Smile: A friendly smile can go a long way. It makes you appear approachable and pleasant.

- Natural Expressions: Use photos where you look relaxed and natural, avoiding overly posed or forced smiles.

C. Include a Variety of Shots

1. Diverse Images:

- Variety: Show different facets of your life and personality. Include photos of you in different settings and doing various activities.

- Balanced Representation: Combine casual photos with more formal ones to give a well-rounded view of yourself.

2. Active and Social:

- Hobbies: Include photos that highlight your hobbies and interests, such as hiking, cooking, or playing an instrument.

- Social Interactions: Show yourself interacting with friends or family to indicate your social life.

D. Avoid Group Photos

1. Clear Identification:

- Stand Out: Ensure you stand out in any group photos. If you include group photos, make sure it's clear who you are in the picture.

- Highlighting Yourself: Position yourself prominently in the group photo to avoid confusion.

2. Solo Shots:

- Individual Focus: Prioritize individual photos to avoid confusion. Solo shots ensure that potential matches know exactly who they are looking at.

E. Be Authentic

1. True Representation:

- Realistic: Show how you look in everyday situations. Avoid overly glamorous or staged photos that don't represent your daily appearance.

- Genuine: Choose photos that genuinely reflect your personality and lifestyle.

2. Minimal Editing:

- Natural Look: Avoid heavy filters or excessive editing. Too much editing can make you appear different from your real self.

- Authenticity: Strive for authenticity and honesty in your photos.

F. Update Regularly

1. Current Images:

- Fresh Photos: Regularly refresh your photos to reflect your current look. Outdated photos can be misleading.

- Recent: Use photos taken within the last year to ensure accuracy.

2. Accurate Depiction:

- True to Self: Ensure your photos match your present self. This builds trust and sets accurate expectations for potential matches.

- Consistency: Regular updates keep your profile active and engaging.

By following these guidelines, you can choose the right photos that effectively showcase your personality, interests, and appearance, enhancing your chances of making meaningful connections.

7.3 Communicating Effectively Online

Effective online communication is essential for building connections and moving towards in-person meetings. Here's how to communicate effectively online:

A. Start with a Strong Opening Message

1. Personalized Approach:

- Tailored Messages: Tailor your messages to the person's interests. Reference something specific from their profile to show you've taken the time to read it.

- Unique Starters: Avoid generic openers. For example, instead of "Hey," say, "I noticed you love hiking – what's your favorite trail?"

2. Thoughtful Engagement:

- Genuine Interest: Show genuine interest in their profile. Ask about their hobbies, interests, or something unique they mentioned.

- Positive Tone: Start with a positive and friendly tone to set the stage for a pleasant conversation.

B. Be Respectful and Polite

1. Courtesy:

- Respectful Tone: Maintain a respectful tone in all interactions. Use polite language and avoid being overly familiar too soon.

- Consideration: Be considerate of their feelings and boundaries.

2. Appropriate Humor:

- Tasteful Jokes: Use humor carefully and appropriately. Light-hearted jokes can break the ice, but avoid sarcasm or humor that could be misinterpreted.

- Gauge Response: Pay attention to how they respond to humor and adjust accordingly.

C. Ask Open-Ended Questions

1. Engaging Questions:

- Conversation Starters: Foster deeper conversations with thoughtful, open-ended questions. Questions like, "What inspired you to travel to Japan?" encourage detailed responses.

- Encourage Sharing: Open-ended questions invite them to share more about themselves.

2. Genuine Curiosity:

- Interest in Their Life: Show interest in getting to know them better. Ask about their passions, experiences, and aspirations.

- Follow-Up Questions: Use follow-up questions to keep the conversation flowing and show that you're actively listening.

D. Share About Yourself

1. Two-Way Dialogue:

- Balance the Conversation: Share insights about yourself to keep the conversation balanced. Avoid dominating the conversation or being too reserved.

- Reciprocity: If they share a personal story, reciprocate with a similar experience or insight.

2. Personal Insights:

- Interesting Details: Provide interesting details about your life and interests. Share stories that highlight your personality and what makes you unique.

- Authenticity: Be honest and genuine in what you share.

E. Use Proper Grammar and Spelling

1. Attention to Detail:

- Proofreading: Proofread your messages before sending. Correct grammar and spelling show attention to detail and respect for the other person.

- Clear Communication: Well-written messages are easier to read and understand.

2. Professionalism:

- Polished Messages: Well-written messages reflect well on you and demonstrate that you care about making a good impression.

- Consistency: Maintain a consistent level of professionalism in your communication.

F. Be Patient

1. Patience and Understanding:

- Respect Response Time: Respect their response time and avoid appearing pushy. Understand that everyone has different schedules and commitments.

- No Pressure: Avoid sending multiple messages if they haven't replied yet. Give them space to respond.

2. Respectful Follow-Ups:

- Thoughtful Reminders: Follow up thoughtfully if necessary, without pressure. A simple, "Just wanted to check if you saw my last message" can be enough.

- Gentle Persistence: If they haven't responded in a while, a polite follow-up can show continued interest without coming across as pushy.

By following these guidelines, you can communicate effectively online, fostering meaningful connections and paving the way for successful in-person meetings.

7.4 Safety Tips for Online Dating

Safety should always be a priority when engaging in online dating. Here are essential safety tips to keep in mind:

A. Protect Your Personal Information

1. Maintain Privacy:

- Selective Sharing: Keep sensitive information private until trust is established. Avoid sharing your full name, address, workplace, and other personal details too soon.

- Anonymity: Use the platform's anonymity features where available to protect your identity initially.

2. Financial Safety:

- Guard Financial Details: Never share financial details with online matches. Be wary of anyone who asks for money or financial information.

B. Use the Platform's Messaging System

1. App Messaging:

- Initial Communications: Utilize the app's messaging features for initial communications. This keeps your personal contact information private until you feel comfortable.

- Monitoring: App messaging systems often have safety measures in place to monitor for suspicious activity.

2. Security Layers:

- Extra Security: Rely on in-app messaging to safeguard your personal information. Avoid moving to personal email or phone until you're certain of the person's credibility.

C. Trust Your Instincts

1. Listen to Gut Feelings:

- Red Flags: Pay attention to any red flags or discomfort you feel during interactions. If something doesn't feel right, it probably isn't.

- Boundaries: Respect your own boundaries and prioritize your comfort and safety at all times.

2. Cautious Approach:

- Safety First: Always err on the side of caution. If a conversation or interaction feels off, don't hesitate to end it.

D. Do a Background Check

1. Verify Identity:

- Confirm Details: Use available information to confirm their identity. Cross-check details they provide with what you can find online.

- Profile Consistency: Ensure their online presence (social media, LinkedIn, etc.) matches the information they've shared.

2. Online Research:

- Search Engines: Conduct basic online searches to ensure credibility. Look for any signs of deception or concerning behavior.

E. Meet in Public Places

1. Public Venues:

- Safe Locations: Choose safe, public locations for initial meetings, such as cafes, restaurants, or parks. Avoid private or secluded places.

- Accessibility: Pick places that are easily accessible and have good lighting and visibility.

2. Safety Check-Ins:

- Inform Contacts: Keep friends or family informed about your whereabouts and who you're meeting. Share your location and check in with them before, during, and after the date.

F. Have a Safety Plan

1. Independent Transportation:

- Control Travel: Ensure you have control over your travel arrangements. Drive yourself or use a rideshare service, so you're not reliant on your date for transportation.

- Exit Strategy: Have a plan for how to leave if you feel uncomfortable.

2. Safety Contacts:

- Trusted Contact: Designate a trusted contact for check-ins during dates. Share your plans and have them check in with you at agreed times.

- Emergency Plan: Have a code word or signal to use with your contact in case you need help.

G. Be Cautious with Photos and Social Media

1. Privacy Settings:

- Profile Privacy: Adjust social media settings to protect your privacy. Limit who can see your posts and personal information.

- Limited Sharing: Be cautious about linking social media profiles to dating profiles.

2. Discretion in Sharing:

- Selective Posting: Avoid posting identifiable or location-specific photos that could be used to find you.

- Safety in Images: Choose photos that maintain a level of privacy about your exact location and daily routines.

By following these safety tips, you can protect yourself while engaging in online dating. Prioritize your safety and comfort, use the platform's features wisely, and trust your instincts to ensure a secure and positive dating experience.

Chapter 7 Review: Creating an Attractive Profile

Creating an attractive profile is crucial for success in online dating. This chapter covers how to craft a compelling bio, choose the right photos, communicate effectively online, and follow essential safety tips.

7.1 Crafting a Compelling Bio

- Be Authentic: Represent yourself accurately by highlighting your true interests, values, and what you're looking for in a relationship.

- Showcase Your Personality: Use a conversational tone, include humor, and mention hobbies, passions, and unique quirks.

- Keep It Concise: Write a few well-crafted sentences or a short paragraph that covers the most important aspects of who you are.

- Include a Call to Action: Encourage potential matches to reach out by inviting them to connect based on shared interests.

- Be Positive: Focus on what you enjoy and avoid mentioning negative experiences.

- Proofread: Ensure your bio is polished and free of spelling and grammar errors.

7.2 Choosing the Right Photos

- Use High-Quality Images: Ensure your photos are clear and well-lit to create a good impression.

- Show Your Face: Use a recent photo of your face as your main profile picture and smile to appear approachable.

- Include a Variety of Shots: Use a mix of photos that show different aspects of your life, such as hobbies, activities, and social interactions.

- Avoid Group Photos: Ensure you are easily identifiable in any group photos or prioritize solo shots.

- Be Authentic: Use photos that represent how you look day-to-day without excessive editing.

- Update Regularly: Keep your photos current to reflect your present appearance and lifestyle.

7.3 Communicating Effectively Online

- Start with a Strong Opening Message: Personalize your messages based on the person's profile to show genuine interest.

- Be Respectful and Polite: Maintain courtesy and avoid inappropriate comments or jokes.

- Ask Open-Ended Questions: Encourage deeper conversations by asking questions that require more than a yes or no answer.

- Share About Yourself: Balance your questions with information about yourself to create a two-way conversation.

- Use Proper Grammar and Spelling: Good grammar and spelling make a positive impression and show effort.

- Be Patient: Give your matches time to respond and avoid sending multiple messages if you don't get an immediate reply.

7.4 Safety Tips for Online Dating

- Protect Your Personal Information: Avoid sharing details like your home address, phone number, or financial information with someone you've just met online.

- Use the Platform's Messaging System: Keep initial conversations within the dating app's messaging system for added security.

- Trust Your Instincts: If something feels off or uncomfortable, trust your instincts and proceed with caution or discontinue communication.

- Do a Background Check: Verify their identity through basic online research before meeting in person.

- Meet in Public Places: Always arrange first dates in public locations and inform a friend or family member of your plans.

- Have a Safety Plan: Arrange your own transportation and have a friend you can call if you feel unsafe.

- Be Cautious with Photos and Social Media: Be mindful of what you share online and adjust your privacy settings to protect your personal information.

Summary

This chapter provides essential guidance for creating an attractive and safe online dating profile. By crafting a compelling bio, selecting the right photos, communicating effectively, and following safety tips, you can enhance your online dating experience and increase your chances of finding a meaningful connection.

Chapter 8: Meeting People Offline

In an era dominated by digital interactions, meeting people offline can seem daunting, but it remains one of the most genuine and rewarding ways to form connections. Face-to-face interactions provide a depth and authenticity that online platforms often lack. This chapter will explore strategies for expanding your social circle, attending social events and gatherings, approaching and talking to strangers, and utilizing mutual connections to enhance your dating and relationship prospects.

8.1 Expanding Your Social Circle

Expanding your social circle is the first step to meeting new people and potential partners. A broad and diverse network can provide numerous opportunities to connect with like-minded individuals. Here are effective strategies to help you grow your social circle:

A. Join Clubs and Groups

1. Shared Interests:

- Aligned Hobbies: Engage in clubs and groups that align with your hobbies and passions. This could be anything from book clubs and sports teams to cooking classes and volunteer organizations.

- Common Ground: Joining groups based on shared interests naturally provides conversation starters and common ground for building relationships.

2. Consistent Participation:

- Regular Attendance: Regularly attend meetings and events to build rapport and establish a presence within the group.

- Active Involvement: Volunteer for roles within the group, such as organizing events or leading activities, to increase your visibility and involvement.

B. Attend Workshops and Seminars

1. Professional Development:

- Career-Oriented Events: Look for workshops and seminars related to your career or personal interests. These events provide an excellent platform to meet people with similar aspirations.

- Learning Opportunities: Engage in activities that can enhance your skills and knowledge while providing networking opportunities.

2. Networking Opportunities:

- Social Interactions: Take advantage of networking sessions during these events to introduce yourself and exchange contact information.

- Follow-Up: After the event, follow up with new contacts through email or social media to maintain and strengthen connections.

C. Volunteer for Causes You Care About

1. Community Engagement:

- Meaningful Causes: Volunteering is a great way to meet people who share your values and interests. Choose causes that resonate with you to ensure meaningful interactions.

- Shared Goals: Working together towards a common goal fosters a sense of camaraderie and mutual respect.

2. Regular Involvement:

- Commitment: Commit to volunteering regularly to form lasting connections with fellow volunteers.

- Event Participation: Participate in or help organize volunteer events, which can provide additional opportunities to meet new people.

D. Take Up New Hobbies

1. Exploration:

- New Activities: Explore new hobbies and activities that interest you. This not only broadens your horizons but also introduces you to new social circles.

- Variety: Trying diverse activities increases the likelihood of meeting a wide range of people.

2. Skill Development:

- Personal Growth: Hobbies like dancing, cooking, or hiking can enhance your personal development while providing opportunities to meet others.

- Class Participation: Enroll in classes or workshops related to your hobbies to meet people with similar interests.

E. Socialize at Work

1. Workplace Relationships:

- Beyond Work: Engage with colleagues beyond work-related interactions. Attend office parties, join workplace clubs, and participate in team-building activities.

- Common Interests: Find out if any colleagues share your interests and suggest activities or events you can do together.

2. After-Work Events:

- Relaxed Settings: Take part in after-work social events to connect with colleagues in a more relaxed setting.

- Building Bonds: Use these opportunities to build stronger relationships and expand your social circle within the professional environment.

By implementing these strategies, you can effectively expand your social circle, creating more opportunities to meet potential partners and forge meaningful connections.

8.2 Attending Social Events and Gatherings

Social events and gatherings are prime opportunities to meet new people and potential partners. Here's how to make the most of these occasions:

A. Be Open and Approachable

1. Positive Body Language:

- Smile: A genuine smile can make you appear more friendly and approachable.

- Eye Contact: Maintain eye contact to show interest and confidence.

- Open Posture: Avoid crossing your arms and maintain an open posture to appear more welcoming.

2. *Initiate Conversations:*

- Start Small: Take the initiative to start conversations with people you don't know. Simple openers like, "Hi, I'm [Your Name], how do you know the host?" can be very effective.

- Show Interest: Ask open-ended questions to keep the conversation flowing and show genuine interest in the other person.

B. Attend a Variety of Events

1. *Diverse Activities:*

- Mix of Events: Attend a mix of formal and informal events, such as parties, cultural events, festivals, and community gatherings. This variety increases your chances of meeting different kinds of people.

- Explore New Venues: Don't be afraid to step out of your comfort zone and explore new types of events.

2. *Frequent Attendance:*

- Consistency: Regularly attend different types of events to increase your chances of meeting new people. Becoming a familiar face can also help in building rapport.

- Expand Horizons: The more events you attend, the more opportunities you have to expand your social network.

C. Leverage Your Interests

1. *Interest-Based Events:*

- Aligned Events: Focus on events that align with your interests and passions. This ensures you meet people with similar likes and values.

- Common Ground: Having common interests provides a natural starting point for conversations and connections.

2. Active Participation:

- Engage Fully: Engage actively in the event activities to increase your visibility and opportunities for interaction. Participate in group activities, discussions, or any interactive segments.

- Volunteering: Offer to help with event activities or organization to meet people in a more involved setting.

D. Network Strategically

1. Targeted Networking:

- Identify Key Individuals: Identify key individuals you'd like to meet and seek opportunities to connect with them. This could be event organizers, speakers, or other attendees.

- Approach Confidently: Approach these individuals confidently and introduce yourself. Have a few conversation starters ready to ease the interaction.

2. Follow Up:

- Maintain Contact: After the event, follow up with new contacts to nurture the relationship. Send a friendly message or connect on social media.

- Regular Check-Ins: Keep in touch periodically to maintain and strengthen the connection.

E. Bring a Friend

1. Support System:

- Confidence Boost: Bringing a friend can boost your confidence and make it easier to approach new people. Friends can provide moral support and make the experience more enjoyable.

- Wingman Effect: Having a friend with you can help in starting conversations and easing into social circles.

2. Expand Networks:

- Introductions: Your friends can introduce you to their acquaintances, further expanding your social circle. This can lead to meeting people you wouldn't have encountered otherwise.

- Shared Connections: Shared connections can provide a comfortable bridge to new social groups.

By being open and approachable, attending a variety of events, leveraging your interests, networking strategically, and bringing a friend, you can effectively use social events and gatherings to expand your social circle and meet potential partners.

8.3 Approaching and Talking to Strangers

Approaching and talking to strangers can be intimidating, but it's a crucial skill for meeting new people. Here's how to do it effectively:

A. Overcome Initial Hesitation

1. Positive Mindset:

- Optimism: Adopt a positive attitude and remind yourself of the potential benefits of meeting new people. Focus on the opportunities for new friendships and connections rather than the fear of rejection.

- Affirmations: Use positive affirmations to boost your confidence. Remind yourself that meeting new people can lead to exciting experiences and opportunities.

2. Small Steps:

- Simple Interactions: Start with small interactions, like greeting a neighbor or making small talk with a cashier. These low-pressure situations can help build your confidence.

- Gradual Progression: Gradually increase the length and depth of your conversations as you become more comfortable.

B. Use Openers and Icebreakers

1. Compliments:

- Genuine Praise: Offer a genuine compliment to break the ice. Compliments can make people feel appreciated and open to conversation.

- Positive Observations: Comment on something you genuinely like about their appearance, actions, or belongings, such as "I love your jacket!" or "You did a great job on that presentation."

2. Common Interests:

- Shared Topics: Mention shared interests or comment on the event or environment to start a conversation. For example, "This is a great event, have you been here before?" or "I see you're reading [book title], how are you liking it so far?"

C. Practice Active Listening

1. Show Interest:

- Attentive Listening: Listen attentively and show genuine interest in what the other person is saying. Nod, smile, and use verbal affirmations like "I see" or "That's interesting."

- Eye Contact: Maintain eye contact to show that you are engaged and interested in the conversation.

2. Follow-Up Questions:

- Engaging Questions: Ask open-ended questions to keep the conversation flowing. Questions like "What do you enjoy most about [topic]?" or "Can you tell me more about [subject]?" encourage deeper discussions.

- Building on Responses: Build on their responses to demonstrate that you are actively listening and interested in their thoughts.

D. Be Confident and Authentic

1. Confidence:

- Self-Assurance: Approach others with confidence and a friendly demeanor. Stand tall, make eye contact, and speak clearly.

- Positive Energy: Project positive energy to make others feel comfortable and open to engaging with you.

2. Authenticity:

- Be Yourself: Be yourself and avoid trying to impress others with exaggerated stories or achievements. Authenticity fosters genuine connections.

- Honesty: Share your true thoughts and feelings, which helps build trust and rapport.

E. Respect Boundaries

1. Personal Space:

- Physical Boundaries: Be mindful of personal space and body language cues. Respect the other person's comfort zone and avoid getting too close too quickly.

- Nonverbal Signals: Pay attention to nonverbal signals that indicate whether the person is comfortable or not.

2. Exit Gracefully:

- Polite Departure: If the conversation isn't going well, exit gracefully with a polite excuse. For example, "It was nice talking to you, but I need to go catch up with a friend."

- Gracious Exit: Thank them for the conversation and wish them well.

F. Practice Makes Perfect

1. Repetition:

- Consistent Practice: The more you practice approaching and talking to strangers, the more comfortable it will become. Aim to engage in new conversations regularly.

- Confidence Building: Each successful interaction builds your confidence and makes future encounters easier.

2. *Learn from Experience:*

- Reflective Learning: Reflect on your interactions and learn from both successful and unsuccessful attempts. Consider what worked well and what you could improve for next time.

- Continuous Improvement: Use feedback from your experiences to continuously improve your social skills.

By overcoming initial hesitation, using effective openers and icebreakers, practicing active listening, being confident and authentic, respecting boundaries, and continually practicing, you can become more comfortable and skilled at approaching and talking to strangers.

8.4 Utilizing Mutual Connections

Utilizing mutual connections can be an effective way to meet new people, as introductions through friends or acquaintances often come with a built-in level of trust. Here's how to leverage mutual connections:

A. Let Your Network Know

1. Express Interest:

- Open Communication: Inform your friends and family that you're open to meeting new people and interested in being introduced. Make sure they know you are actively looking to expand your social circle.

- Clear Intentions: Be clear about whether you're looking for friendships, professional connections, or potential romantic relationships.

2. Be Specific:

- Desired Traits: Share the type of people you're looking to meet. Provide specific traits or interests you find appealing, which helps your network make more suitable introductions.

- Contextual Relevance: Mention any particular contexts or settings where you'd prefer to meet new people.

B. Attend Gatherings with Mutual Connections

1. Social Invitations:

- Accept Invitations: Accept invitations to events hosted by friends or acquaintances where you can meet their social circle. These gatherings often provide a relaxed environment conducive to meeting new people.

- Networking Mindset: Approach these events with the intention of meeting new people and expanding your network.

2. Engage Actively:

- Participate Fully: Participate in group activities and conversations to maximize your interactions. Show genuine interest in getting to know the people you meet.

- Positive Presence: Be approachable and friendly, making it easier for others to engage with you.

C. Ask for Introductions

1. Direct Requests:

- Proactive Approach: Don't hesitate to ask friends to introduce you to someone they think you'd get along with. A direct request can often lead to meaningful introductions.

- Comfortable Settings: Choose settings where both parties are likely to feel comfortable and open to meeting new people.

2. Contextual Introductions:

- Appropriate Settings: Request introductions in appropriate settings, such as social gatherings, casual meetups, or even online social media platforms.

- Smooth Transitions: Ensure the introduction is seamless and natural, making the new connection feel at ease.

D. Follow Up on Introductions

1. Show Appreciation:

- Gratitude: Thank the mutual connection for the introduction and express your gratitude. This reinforces the relationship with your mutual connection and shows your appreciation for their effort.

- Positive Feedback: Provide feedback about the introduction to keep your mutual connection informed.

2. Initiate Contact:

- Reach Out: Reach out to the new contact and suggest a casual meetup or activity. A simple message like, "It was great meeting you at [event], would you like to grab coffee sometime?" can go a long way.

- Plan Activities: Suggest engaging activities that reflect shared interests to build rapport.

E. Maintain and Nurture Connections

1. Regular Communication:

- Consistent Contact: Keep in touch with both your mutual connection and the new contact to build a strong relationship. Regular check-ins can help maintain and deepen these connections.

- Shared Activities: Plan regular meetups or activities that can strengthen the bond over time.

2. Support and Reciprocity:

- Mutual Support: Offer support and be willing to reciprocate introductions and favors. Helping others in your network can foster goodwill and strengthen your relationships.

- Building Trust: Demonstrate reliability and trustworthiness to nurture these connections.

By letting your network know your intentions, actively attending gatherings, asking for introductions, following up, and maintaining these connections, you can effectively utilize mutual connections to expand your social circle and meet potential partners.

Chapter 8 Review: Meeting People Offline

Meeting people offline is essential for building authentic and meaningful connections. This chapter focuses on expanding your social circle, attending social events, confidently approaching strangers, and utilizing mutual connections.

8.1 Expanding Your Social Circle

- Pursue Interests and Hobbies: Join clubs, groups, or classes related to your passions, such as sports, art, or music.

- Volunteer: Engage in community service to meet like-minded individuals who share your values.

- Attend Networking Events: Participate in professional gatherings to connect with people in your industry.

- Reconnect with Old Friends: Reestablish connections with past friends to broaden your social network.

- Be Open to New Experiences: Accept invitations and try new activities to meet diverse individuals.

- Host Social Gatherings: Organize events like dinner parties or game nights to bring different groups of friends together.

8.2 Attending Social Events and Gatherings

- Choose the Right Events: Attend events that align with your interests to meet like-minded people.

- Be Approachable: Use positive body language, smile, and make eye contact to appear friendly.

- Engage in Conversations: Start with open-ended questions and show genuine interest in others' responses.

- Show Genuine Interest: Listen actively and share your experiences to build rapport.

- Network Strategically: Prepare a brief introduction and be ready to exchange contact information.

- Participate Actively: Get involved in event activities and games to become more noticeable.

8.3 Approaching and Talking to Strangers

- Start with a Smile: Use a warm smile to set a positive tone for the interaction.

- Use Openers: Begin conversations with simple and friendly openers like "Hi, I'm [Your Name]. What brings you here?"

- Find Common Ground: Discuss shared interests or experiences to create a connection.

- Practice Active Listening: Show engagement by listening attentively and responding thoughtfully.

- Be Confident: Project confidence through your body language and speech.

- Know When to Move On: Politely excuse yourself if the conversation isn't flowing naturally.

8.4 Utilizing Mutual Connections

- Ask for Introductions: Request friends or acquaintances to introduce you to people you're interested in meeting.

- Attend Group Activities: Join group outings organized by your friends for a comfortable environment to meet new people.

- Be a Connector: Introduce your friends to each other, which can expand your network and encourage reciprocation.

- Use Social Media: Leverage platforms like LinkedIn and Facebook to identify mutual connections and arrange introductions.

- Participate in Community Events: Attend events hosted by your mutual connections to meet individuals with common interests.

Summary

Meeting people offline involves expanding your social circle, attending social events, confidently approaching and talking to strangers, and utilizing mutual connections. By actively engaging in these strategies, you can increase your chances of meeting potential partners and building meaningful connections. This chapter provides practical, step-by-step guidance to help you navigate the offline dating landscape with confidence and success.

Chapter 9: The First Date

The first date is a critical step in the dating process. It's the opportunity to make a great first impression, get to know each other, and determine if there's potential for a future relationship. This chapter provides comprehensive guidance on planning the perfect first date, making a great first impression, communicating effectively, and evaluating compatibility.

9.1 Planning the Perfect First Date

Planning the perfect first date sets the tone for a potential relationship. A well-thought-out date shows effort and consideration, helping to create a memorable experience. Here's how to plan the perfect first date:

A. Choose the Right Venue

1. Coffee Shops:

- Casual and Relaxed: Great for a relaxed, casual setting where you can talk without pressure.

- Easy Exit: If the date isn't going well, it's easy to cut it short without awkwardness.

2. Casual Restaurants:

- Comfortable Dining: Ideal for a comfortable meal without too much formality. Choose a place with a varied menu to cater to different tastes.

- Atmosphere: Opt for a restaurant with a pleasant ambiance that encourages conversation.

3. Parks:

- Romantic Walks: A walk in the park can be romantic and offers plenty of opportunities for conversation.

- Natural Beauty: Nature can create a serene backdrop, making the date more enjoyable.

4. Activity Venues:

- Interactive Fun: Places like mini-golf, bowling, or museums provide built-in conversation starters and keep things fun.

- Shared Experiences: Engaging in activities can ease nerves and create shared memories.

B. Consider Interests and Preferences

1. Personalized Planning:

- Know Their Interests: Tailoring the date to their interests shows attentiveness and thoughtfulness. If they love art, a visit to an art gallery could be perfect.

- Shared Hobbies: If you both enjoy a particular hobby, incorporate it into the date for a more personalized experience.

C. Plan for Comfort

1. Accessibility:

- Convenient Location: Choose a location that's easy for both of you to get to. Consider proximity to public transport or parking availability.

- Safety: Ensure the venue is in a safe and well-lit area.

2. Comfortable Setting:

- Relaxed Environment: Pick a place where you can both relax and enjoy the time together. Avoid places that are too noisy or crowded.

- Seating: Comfortable seating arrangements can make a big difference in how at ease you both feel.

D. Keep It Simple

1. Simplicity:

- Focus on Connection: A simple setting often allows for better conversation and connection. Avoid overly elaborate plans that could cause stress.

- Ease of Interaction: Simpler venues enable you to focus on getting to know each other without distractions.

E. Have a Backup Plan

1. Flexibility:

- Plan B: Having a backup plan shows foresight and adaptability. If your first choice doesn't work out, you'll have another option ready.

- Weather Considerations: For outdoor dates, have an indoor alternative in case of bad weather.

F. Set a Time Limit

1. Manage Expectations:

- Defined Timeframe: A defined timeframe can help alleviate pressure and make both parties feel more comfortable. It's easier to extend a date that's going well than to cut one short.

- Casual Commitment: A shorter initial meeting, like coffee, can be less intimidating and more manageable.

By considering these factors, you can plan a first date that is thoughtful, comfortable, and enjoyable, setting the stage for a potential relationship.

9.2 Making a Great First Impression

First impressions are crucial and can set the stage for future interactions. Here's how to make a great first impression:

A. Be Punctual

- Timeliness: Arriving on time demonstrates reliability and respect for the other person's time. It shows that you value the date and are considerate of their schedule.

- Preparation: Plan your route and allow for potential delays to ensure punctuality.

B. Dress Appropriately

- Appropriate Attire: Dressing well shows effort and respect for the occasion. Choose attire that is suitable for the venue and activity.

- Personal Style: While dressing appropriately, also ensure you feel comfortable and confident in what you're wearing.

C. Greet Warmly

- Warm Welcome: A friendly greeting sets a positive tone for the date. A smile, eye contact, and a warm "Hello" can go a long way.

- Handshake or Hug: Depending on your comfort level and cultural norms, a handshake or a brief hug can also help break the ice.

D. Show Genuine Interest

- Engagement: Pay close attention to what your date is saying and show genuine interest in their responses. Nod, make affirming noises, and respond thoughtfully.

- Follow-Up Questions: Ask follow-up questions that show you're engaged and interested in learning more about them.

E. Maintain Positive Body Language

- Body Language: Maintain an open and relaxed posture. Avoid crossing your arms or looking away frequently.

- Eye Contact: Maintain appropriate eye contact to show you are engaged and confident.

- Facial Expressions: Use positive facial expressions, like smiling, to convey friendliness and warmth.

F. Be Yourself

- Authenticity: Being genuine helps establish a real connection. Don't try to be someone you're not just to impress your date.

- Honest Communication: Share your true thoughts and feelings, and be honest about your interests and experiences.

By following these guidelines, you can make a great first impression, setting a positive tone for the rest of your date and paving the way for future interactions.

9.3 Effective Communication on a Date

Effective communication is essential for a successful first date. It helps both parties feel understood and connected. Here are some tips for effective communication on a date:

A. Start with Light Conversation

- Ice Breakers: Light conversation topics ease into more meaningful discussions. Start with simple subjects like hobbies, recent activities, or favorite movies.

- Comfortable Atmosphere: Light conversation helps create a relaxed and comfortable atmosphere, making it easier to transition to deeper topics.

B. Ask Open-Ended Questions

- Engaging Questions: Open-ended questions foster deeper conversation. Instead of asking yes/no questions, try "What do you enjoy most about your job?" or "How do you like to spend your weekends?"

- Personal Insights: These questions encourage your date to share more about themselves, providing valuable insights into their personality and interests.

C. Share About Yourself

- Balanced Sharing: Equal sharing builds a mutual connection. Share your thoughts and experiences, but also give your date ample opportunity to speak.

- Personal Stories: Share personal stories and experiences that highlight your personality and values, helping to build a deeper connection.

D. Listen Actively

- Active Listening: Demonstrates engagement and interest. Show that you are listening by nodding, maintaining eye contact, and responding appropriately.

- Reflect and Respond: Reflect back what your date has said and respond thoughtfully, which shows that you value their input.

E. Avoid Controversial Topics

- Neutral Topics: Stick to safe topics that help build a positive connection. Avoid controversial subjects like politics, religion, or contentious social issues on the first date.

- Positive Focus: Keep the conversation positive and enjoyable, focusing on shared interests and experiences.

F. Be Respectful

- Respect and Empathy: Foster a respectful and understanding atmosphere. Respect your date's opinions and feelings, even if they differ from your own.

- Empathy: Show empathy and consideration for their perspectives, creating a foundation of mutual respect and understanding.

By following these guidelines for effective communication on a date, you can create a comfortable and engaging environment that fosters connection and understanding. This sets the stage for a successful first date and potential future interactions.

9.4 Evaluating Compatibility

Evaluating compatibility on a first date involves observing both your interactions and your feelings. Here's how to assess whether there's potential for a future relationship:

A. Assess Conversation Flow

- Natural Flow: Smooth conversation suggests mutual interest. Pay attention to whether the conversation flows naturally without awkward pauses.

- Engagement: Notice if both of you are equally engaged in the conversation, contributing and responding with interest.

B. Observe Body Language

- Positive Cues: Positive body language, such as leaning in, maintaining eye contact, and smiling, indicates comfort and interest.

- Mirroring: Observe if your date mirrors your body language, which is often a sign of rapport and connection.

C. Consider Shared Interests and Values

- Common Ground: Identify common interests and activities that you both enjoy. Shared hobbies and passions can strengthen the bond between you.

- Values Alignment: Discuss values and life goals to see if they align. Similar values are crucial for long-term compatibility.

D. Evaluate Emotional Connection

- Feeling Understood: A strong emotional bond is essential. Pay attention to whether you feel understood and emotionally connected during your conversations.

- Empathy and Understanding: Notice if your date shows empathy and understanding towards your feelings and experiences.

E. Check Your Comfort Level

- Relaxed Atmosphere: Comfort with each other indicates good compatibility. Assess whether you feel at ease and relaxed in your date's company.

- Natural Interaction: Consider if your interactions feel natural and effortless, without forcing conversation or behavior.

F. Reflect on Red Flags

- Early Recognition: Early recognition of red flags can prevent future issues. Pay attention to any signs of disrespect, dishonesty, or incompatible behavior.

- Trust Your Gut: Trust your instincts and gut feelings. If something feels off, it's important to acknowledge and address it.

By evaluating these aspects during your first date, you can gain a better understanding of your compatibility and determine if there's potential for a future relationship. This careful assessment helps ensure that you invest your time and energy in connections that have the promise of growth and fulfillment.

Chapter 9 Review: The First Date

The first date is a crucial step in the dating process, setting the tone for a potential relationship. This chapter offers comprehensive guidance on planning the perfect first date, making a great first impression, communicating effectively, and evaluating compatibility.

9.1 Planning the Perfect First Date

- Choosing the Right Venue: Opt for comfortable, conversation-friendly locations like coffee shops, casual restaurants, parks, or activity venues such as mini-golf or museums.

- Consider Interests and Preferences: Tailor the date to your partner's interests to show attentiveness and thoughtfulness.

- Plan for Comfort: Ensure the venue is easily accessible and comfortable, avoiding overly loud or crowded places.

- Keep It Simple: Focus on creating an environment for getting to know each other without overcomplicating things.

- Have a Backup Plan: Be prepared with an alternative plan for unforeseen circumstances.

- Set a Time Limit: A shorter date with the option to extend helps manage expectations and alleviate pressure.

9.2 Making a Great First Impression

- Be Punctual: Arrive on time to show respect and reliability.

- Dress Appropriately: Choose attire suitable for the venue that makes you feel confident.

- Greet Warmly: Use a genuine smile and friendly greeting to set a positive tone.

- Show Genuine Interest: Engage actively by asking questions and listening attentively.

- Maintain Positive Body Language: Use open and inviting body language to convey interest and engagement.

- Be Yourself: Authenticity is key to building a genuine connection.

9.3 Effective Communication on a Date

- Start with Light Conversation: Break the ice with easy, everyday topics before moving to deeper subjects.

- Ask Open-Ended Questions: Encourage sharing by asking questions that require more than a yes or no answer.

- Share About Yourself: Balance the conversation by sharing your interests and experiences.

- Listen Actively: Show engagement through nodding, eye contact, and appropriate responses.

- Avoid Controversial Topics: Steer clear of potentially divisive subjects like politics or religion.

- Be Respectful: Respect your date's opinions and experiences, even if they differ from your own.

9.4 Evaluating Compatibility

- Assess Conversation Flow: Observe if the conversation flows naturally and easily.

- Observe Body Language: Pay attention to positive body language cues indicating comfort and interest.

- Consider Shared Interests and Values: Reflect on whether you have common interests and values.

- Evaluate Emotional Connection: Consider if you felt an emotional connection or spark during the date.

- Check Your Comfort Level: Assess how comfortable and at ease you felt with your date.

- Reflect on Red Flags: Be honest about any red flags or deal-breakers you noticed early on.

Summary

Planning a thoughtful first date, making a great impression, communicating effectively, and evaluating compatibility are essential steps to ensure a successful start to a potential relationship. This chapter provides practical guidance to help you navigate the first date with confidence and increase your chances of a meaningful connection.

Part 4: Building a Relationship

Chapter 10: Early Stages of a Relationship

In the early stages of a relationship, laying a solid foundation is crucial for long-term success. This phase involves understanding the honeymoon period, establishing trust, navigating conflicts, and creating healthy communication patterns. Here's how to build a strong start for a lasting relationship.

10.1 Understanding the Honeymoon Phase

The honeymoon phase is characterized by excitement, intense emotions, and a sense of bliss. Understanding this phase is crucial as it sets the tone for the rest of the relationship. Here's what you need to know:

A. Characteristics of the Honeymoon Phase

- Infatuation and Excitement: The intense attraction and enthusiasm you feel for each other make everything seem perfect. This period is marked by high energy, frequent laughter, and a general feeling of euphoria.

- Frequent Communication: You may find yourselves texting, calling, or meeting up frequently, eager to share every detail of your lives. This constant communication helps build a strong initial connection.

B. Emotional Intensity

- Positive Focus: You tend to see your partner through rose-colored glasses, emphasizing their best qualities and minimizing any negative aspects. This positive bias helps in forming a strong bond.

- Strong Bonding: The emotional highs help establish a deep initial connection, laying the groundwork for a more stable relationship. This intense bonding creates a foundation of trust and affection.

C. Setting Realistic Expectations

- Temporary Nature: Understand that the heightened emotions will eventually level out. Recognizing that the intensity will decrease over time helps manage expectations and avoid disappointment.

- Preparation for Stability: Preparing for this transition can prevent disillusionment when the intensity wanes. Focusing on building a stable, mature relationship during this phase can ease the shift to a more balanced connection.

D. Enjoy the Moment

- Creating Memories: Make the most of this time by creating lasting memories together. Go on adventures, try new activities, and capture moments to look back on fondly.

- Deepening Connection: Use this period to strengthen your emotional bond and understanding of each other. Engage in meaningful conversations and share your dreams, fears, and aspirations to deepen your connection.

Understanding the honeymoon phase and its dynamics helps in building a stronger, more resilient relationship. By appreciating the intensity of this phase while setting realistic expectations and preparing for future stability, you can create a solid foundation for lasting love and companionship.

10.2 Setting the Foundation for Trust

Trust is the cornerstone of any healthy relationship. Establishing trust early on creates a solid foundation for long-term stability. Here's how to set the foundation for trust:

A. Be Honest and Transparent

- Openness: Share your true thoughts and feelings with your partner. Being open fosters a sense of security and closeness.

- Honesty: Avoid hiding information or telling white lies. Complete honesty, even about uncomfortable topics, builds trust.

B. Keep Promises

- Reliability: Demonstrate that you can be counted on. Follow through on commitments to show you are dependable.

- Consistency: Regularly keep your word to build a reputation of trustworthiness. Consistent actions speak louder than words.

C. Communicate Openly

- Express Fears and Hopes: Be open about your vulnerabilities and dreams. Sharing personal aspects of your life fosters deeper understanding and connection.

- Clear Expectations: Clearly state what you expect from the relationship. Mutual understanding of expectations prevents misunderstandings and conflicts.

D. Show Respect

- Boundaries: Honor each other's personal space and limits. Respecting boundaries shows that you value and respect your partner's needs.

- Individuality: Appreciate and respect your partner's unique qualities. Encouraging each other's individuality strengthens the relationship.

E. Be Reliable

- Dependability: Be there for your partner when needed. Showing up during difficult times solidifies trust.

- Support: Offer consistent support through actions. Being a reliable support system enhances the bond of trust.

F. Address Issues Promptly

- Timely Resolution: Address conflicts as they arise to prevent escalation. Promptly dealing with issues shows commitment to the relationship.

- Constructive Approach: Handle disagreements with a focus on resolution and understanding. A constructive approach to conflicts builds mutual respect and trust.

By following these principles, you can establish a strong foundation of trust in your relationship, ensuring long-term stability and deeper connection.

10.3 Navigating Differences and Conflicts

Differences and conflicts are natural in any relationship. Navigating them effectively is key to maintaining harmony and understanding. Here's how to handle differences and conflicts:

A. Acknowledge Differences

- Acceptance: Embrace each other's unique traits and viewpoints. Understand that differing opinions and behaviors are part of what makes each person unique.

- Enrichment: View differences as opportunities for growth and learning. Recognize that your partner's different perspective can enrich your own understanding and experience.

B. Stay Calm and Respectful

- Calm Demeanor: Keep emotions in check during disagreements. Staying calm helps prevent escalation and keeps the conversation productive.

- Issue Focus: Address the problem without attacking your partner. Focus on the specific issue at hand rather than making it personal.

C. Practice Active Listening

- Empathy: Try to understand your partner's perspective. Show empathy by acknowledging their feelings and concerns.

- Non-interruptive Listening: Allow your partner to fully express their thoughts. Listen without interrupting to ensure they feel heard and valued.

D. Seek Common Ground

- Agreement Points: Identify shared goals or values. Finding common ground can help bridge differences and foster collaboration.

- Building Solutions: Use commonalities as a foundation for compromise. Work together to build solutions that address both partners' needs and desires.

E. Compromise and Collaborate

- Give and Take: Be ready to make concessions for the sake of the relationship. Understand that compromise is a necessary part of resolving conflicts.

- Joint Problem-Solving: Work together to find mutually acceptable solutions. Collaboration fosters a sense of partnership and shared responsibility.

F. Take Breaks if Needed

- Cooling-off Period: Step back when necessary to regain composure. Taking a break can prevent heated emotions from dominating the discussion.

- Rational Discussion: Return to the conversation with a clear mind. Approach the issue rationally and with a fresh perspective after a break.

By following these strategies, you can effectively navigate differences and conflicts, fostering a healthier and more harmonious relationship. Understanding and addressing conflicts constructively can strengthen your bond and enhance mutual respect and understanding.

10.4 Establishing Healthy Communication Patterns

Healthy communication is essential for a strong relationship. Establishing effective communication patterns early on sets the stage for long-term success. Here's how to establish healthy communication patterns:

A. Be Clear and Direct

- Clarity: Make your messages clear and straightforward. Avoid ambiguity to ensure your partner understands your thoughts and feelings.

- Directness: State your needs and feelings openly. Being upfront about your desires and concerns fosters transparency and prevents misunderstandings.

B. Use "I" Statements

- Non-Accusatory Language: Frame your feelings in a way that doesn't blame your partner. For example, say "I feel upset when..." instead of "You make me upset when...".

- Personal Responsibility: Take ownership of your emotions. Using "I" statements shows that you are responsible for your own feelings and not blaming your partner.

C. Practice Active Listening

- Engaged Listening: Demonstrate that you are paying attention. Maintain eye contact, nod, and give verbal acknowledgments like "I understand" or "That makes sense."

- Reflection: Paraphrase your partner's words to show comprehension. Reflecting back what they've said confirms that you're listening and provides clarity.

D. Share Positive Feedback

- Appreciation: Express gratitude for your partner's actions and traits. Regularly acknowledge and appreciate the things they do.

- Positive Reinforcement: Highlight and commend positive behaviors. Encouraging good behavior strengthens your bond and promotes a positive atmosphere.

E. Create a Safe Space

- Judgment-Free Zone: Encourage open and honest communication. Make it clear that your partner can share their thoughts and feelings without fear of judgment.

- Emotional Safety: Make your partner feel secure in expressing themselves. Validate their feelings and avoid dismissive or critical responses.

F. Schedule Regular Check-Ins

- Routine Discussions: Set aside time for periodic relationship talks. Regular check-ins provide an opportunity to discuss how things are going and address any issues.

- Issue Resolution: Use these check-ins to address concerns proactively. Regularly discussing the relationship helps prevent small issues from becoming major problems.

G. Be Patient and Understanding

- Patience: Allow time for communication habits to develop. Developing effective communication takes time and practice.

- Mutual Effort: Work together to enhance your communication. Recognize that both partners need to put in effort to improve and maintain healthy communication patterns.

By establishing these healthy communication patterns, you can build a strong foundation for your relationship, ensuring that both partners feel understood, respected, and valued. These practices will help you navigate challenges and maintain a positive and supportive partnership.

Chapter 10 Review: Early Stages of a Relationship

In the early stages of a relationship, laying a solid foundation is crucial for long-term success. This phase involves understanding the honeymoon period, establishing trust, navigating conflicts, and creating healthy communication patterns.

10.1 Understanding the Honeymoon Phase

- Characteristics of the Honeymoon Phase: This phase is marked by infatuation, increased affection, frequent communication, and a desire to spend as much time together as possible.

- Emotional Intensity: Emotions run high, leading to a strong initial bond while often overlooking flaws.

- Setting Realistic Expectations: Recognize that the honeymoon phase is temporary and prepare for the transition to a more stable phase.

- Enjoy the Moment: Embrace the excitement and joy, building memories and deepening your emotional connection.

10.2 Setting the Foundation for Trust

- Be Honest and Transparent: Share your true thoughts and feelings to foster trust and prevent misunderstandings.

- Keep Promises: Follow through on commitments to build reliability and trust.

- Communicate Openly: Discuss experiences, fears, and expectations openly to understand and support each other.

- Show Respect: Respect each other's boundaries, values, and individuality.

- Be Reliable: Demonstrate dependability through actions.

- Address Issues Promptly: Handle conflicts as they arise to prevent erosion of trust.

10.3 Navigating Differences and Conflicts

- Acknowledge Differences: Embrace each other's unique traits and viewpoints.

- Stay Calm and Respectful: Avoid shouting and blaming, focusing instead on resolving the issue.

- Practice Active Listening: Show empathy and understanding during disagreements.

- Seek Common Ground: Identify shared goals or values to build solutions.

- Compromise and Collaborate: Work together to find mutually acceptable solutions.

- Take Breaks if Needed: Step back when necessary to cool down before continuing the conversation.

10.4 Establishing Healthy Communication Patterns

- Be Clear and Direct: Communicate thoughts and feelings clearly and directly.

- Use "I" Statements: Express feelings using non-accusatory language.

- Practice Active Listening: Engage in conversations by nodding, maintaining eye contact, and responding thoughtfully.

- Share Positive Feedback: Regularly express gratitude and commend positive behaviors.

- Create a Safe Space: Foster an environment where both partners feel safe to express themselves.

- Schedule Regular Check-Ins: Discuss the relationship periodically to address any issues and ensure both partners feel valued.

- Be Patient and Understanding: Understand that effective communication takes time and effort, working together to improve.

Summary

The early stages of a relationship are critical for building a strong and lasting foundation. By understanding the honeymoon phase, setting the foundation for trust, navigating differences and conflicts, and establishing healthy communication patterns, you can create a solid and fulfilling relationship. This chapter provides practical, step-by-step guidance to help you navigate the early stages with confidence and ease, ensuring a successful and enduring partnership.

Chapter 11: Developing Trust and Intimacy

Building trust and fostering intimacy are vital for any successful and fulfilling relationship. Trust forms the foundation for emotional safety, open communication, and mutual reliability, while intimacy deepens the emotional and physical connections between partners. This chapter will explore the significance of trust, strategies for building it over time, ways to develop both emotional and physical intimacy, and methods for maintaining healthy boundaries and respect.

11.1 The Importance of Trust in Relationships

Trust is the cornerstone of any healthy and successful relationship. It creates a safe environment where both partners feel secure and valued. Understanding the importance of trust is essential for nurturing a deep and lasting connection:

A. Foundation for Emotional Safety

- Emotional Openness: Trust encourages the sharing of personal thoughts and feelings. When partners trust each other, they feel comfortable being open and honest about their emotions.

- Vulnerability: Builds deeper emotional connections through honest sharing. Trust allows partners to be vulnerable, which strengthens their bond and fosters a sense of closeness.

B. Enhances Communication

- Honest Dialogue: Trust promotes sincere and meaningful conversations. Partners are more likely to speak truthfully and openly when they trust each other.

- Effective Exchange: Improves understanding and reduces misunderstandings. Trust in communication ensures that messages are received as intended, leading to better mutual understanding.

C. Builds Reliability and Dependability

- Consistent Actions: Demonstrates reliability through keeping promises. Consistently following through on commitments reinforces trust.

- Dependable Partner: Strengthens the bond by being a trustworthy presence. Knowing they can rely on each other makes partners feel secure and valued.

D. Supports Conflict Resolution

- Collaborative Approach: Trust focuses on resolving issues together. When trust exists, partners are more likely to work as a team to solve problems.

- Constructive Conflict: Minimizes defensiveness and promotes problem-solving. Trust reduces the fear of being misunderstood or attacked, making conflicts more constructive and less damaging.

E. Promotes Emotional and Physical Intimacy

- Deeper Connection: Trust facilitates closeness and affection. A high level of trust allows partners to connect on a deeper emotional level.

- Intimacy Building: Enhances both emotional and physical bonding. Trust fosters an environment where both emotional and physical intimacy can flourish, leading to a more fulfilling relationship.

By understanding and prioritizing trust, partners can create a stable, loving, and resilient relationship. Trust serves as the foundation upon which all other aspects of the relationship are built, ensuring long-term happiness and connection.

11.2 Building Trust Over Time

Building trust is a gradual process that requires consistent effort and commitment. Here's how to cultivate trust over time:

A. Be Honest and Transparent

- Open Communication: Share your true thoughts and intentions. Being honest about your feelings and intentions fosters an atmosphere of trust.

- Transparency: Foster trust through honesty and openness. Avoid keeping secrets and be forthright about issues that may affect the relationship.

B. Keep Your Promises

- Consistent Reliability: Demonstrate dependability through actions. Follow through on your commitments to show that you can be relied upon.

- Promise Keeping: Strengthen trust by fulfilling commitments. Regularly keeping your word reinforces your partner's confidence in you.

C. Show Respect and Understanding

- Empathetic Listening: Understand and validate your partner's emotions. Listening with empathy shows that you respect their feelings and perspectives.

- Respectful Interaction: Build trust through mutual respect. Treat your partner with consideration and honor their boundaries and needs.

D. *Communicate Openly and Frequently*

- Frequent Dialogue: Keep communication lines open and active. Regular, meaningful conversations help maintain a strong connection.

- Open Sharing: Reduce misunderstandings and build connection. Sharing your thoughts and feelings openly fosters a deeper understanding between you and your partner.

E. *Admit Mistakes and Apologize*

- Accountability: Build trust by owning up to errors. Admitting when you are wrong shows maturity and responsibility.

- Sincere Apologies: Strengthen relationships through genuine remorse. A heartfelt apology can repair trust and demonstrate your commitment to the relationship.

F. *Be Supportive and Reliable*

- Dependable Support: Show up consistently for your partner. Being there during both good and challenging times reinforces trust.

- Reliable Presence: Reinforce trust through consistent actions. Your reliability in everyday situations helps build a solid foundation of trust.

G. *Give Trust to Receive Trust*

- Mutual Trust: Build a trusting relationship by giving trust. Trusting your partner encourages them to trust you in return.

- Reciprocal Trust: Strengthen bonds through mutual trust. A relationship based on mutual trust is more resilient and fulfilling.

By consistently practicing these behaviors, you can build and maintain a strong foundation of trust in your relationship, ensuring long-term stability and deeper connection.

11.3 Developing Emotional and Physical Intimacy

Intimacy is an integral part of a close and fulfilling relationship. It involves emotional closeness as well as physical connection. Here's how to develop both:

A. Emotional Intimacy

- Share Your Feelings: Regularly share your thoughts and emotions with your partner. Open up about your fears, dreams, and experiences. This transparency builds a deeper understanding and connection.

- Practice Active Listening: Listen to your partner without interrupting. Show empathy and understanding, and validate their feelings. This ensures they feel heard and valued.

- Spend Quality Time Together: Make time for each other. Engage in activities that you both enjoy and that foster connection. Shared experiences create lasting memories and strengthen your bond.

- Be Vulnerable: Allow yourself to be vulnerable with your partner. Sharing your innermost thoughts and feelings strengthens emotional intimacy and builds trust.

B. Physical Intimacy

- Communicate About Physical Needs: Discuss your physical needs and preferences openly. Understanding each other's desires enhances physical intimacy and ensures both partners feel satisfied.

- Affectionate Touch: Incorporate affectionate touch into your daily interactions. Holding hands, hugging, and cuddling build physical closeness and convey love and affection.

- Explore Together: Be open to exploring new aspects of physical intimacy together. Communicate openly about your comfort levels and boundaries to ensure a mutually satisfying experience.

- Respect Boundaries: Always respect each other's physical boundaries. Consent and comfort are paramount in physical intimacy, ensuring that both partners feel safe and respected.

Developing both emotional and physical intimacy requires ongoing effort and communication. By prioritizing these aspects of your relationship, you can create a deeper, more fulfilling connection with your partner.

11.4 Maintaining Boundaries and Respect

Boundaries are essential for maintaining a healthy and respectful relationship. They help ensure that both partners feel safe, valued, and respected. Here's how to establish and maintain boundaries:

A. Identify Your Boundaries

- Self-Reflection: Understand your own limits and needs. Take time to reflect on what makes you feel comfortable and what you are willing to accept in your relationship.

- Boundary Identification: Clearly define what makes you comfortable. This might include personal space, time for yourself, and acceptable behaviors.

B. Communicate Clearly

- Open Dialogue: Foster understanding through clear communication. Discuss your boundaries openly with your partner to ensure they understand your needs.

- Mutual Respect: Ensure boundaries are understood and honored. Respect your partner's boundaries as well, creating a foundation of mutual respect.

C. Respect Boundaries Consistently

- Consistent Respect: Build trust through steady boundary respect. Always honor your partner's boundaries to reinforce trust and respect.

- Avoid Overstepping: Honor your partner's comfort levels at all times. Be mindful of their limits and avoid pushing them beyond what they are comfortable with.

D. Revisit Boundaries Regularly

- Ongoing Discussion: Ensure boundaries remain relevant and respected. Regularly check in with your partner to discuss any changes or new boundaries.

- Adaptability: Adjust to changing needs and boundaries. Be flexible and willing to adapt as both your needs evolve over time.

E. Handle Boundary Violations Constructively

- Calm Resolution: Address issues without escalation. If a boundary is crossed, approach the situation calmly and discuss it without anger or blame.

- Constructive Feedback: Discuss violations to prevent recurrence. Provide feedback on why the boundary is important and how to avoid similar issues in the future.

F. Balance Togetherness and Independence

- Individual Space: Maintain personal interests and activities. Ensure that both partners have time for their own hobbies and interests.

- Healthy Balance: Foster both connection and individuality. Balance time spent together with time apart to maintain a healthy and dynamic relationship.

By establishing and maintaining boundaries, you create a respectful and secure environment that allows both partners to thrive individually and together. This foundation of respect and understanding is crucial for a strong and lasting relationship.

Chapter 11 Review: Developing Trust and Intimacy

Chapter 11 focuses on the essential components of building trust and fostering intimacy in relationships. It emphasizes the importance of trust, strategies for cultivating it over time, ways to develop both emotional and physical intimacy, and methods for maintaining healthy boundaries and respect.

11.1 The Importance of Trust in Relationships

- Emotional Safety: Trust enables vulnerability and openness, creating a secure environment.

- Enhanced Communication: Promotes honest and effective dialogue, improving understanding.

- Reliability: Builds a dependable foundation through consistent actions and promise-keeping.

- Conflict Resolution: Facilitates collaborative problem-solving and reduces defensiveness.

- Intimacy: Deepens emotional and physical connections, fostering a stronger bond.

11.2 Building Trust Over Time

- Honesty and Transparency: Share true thoughts, feelings, and intentions openly.

- Keeping Promises: Consistently fulfill commitments to build reliability.

- Respect and Empathy: Show understanding and validate each other's feelings.

- Open Communication: Maintain frequent, honest conversations to prevent misunderstandings.

- Admitting Mistakes: Own up to errors and apologize sincerely to reinforce trust.

- Support and Reliability: Be consistently present and dependable for your partner.

- Reciprocal Trust: Trust your partner to encourage mutual trust and strengthen bonds.

11.3 Developing Emotional and Physical Intimacy

- Emotional Intimacy:

  - Sharing Feelings: Regularly express your thoughts, dreams, and fears.

  - Active Listening: Show empathy and validate each other's feelings.

  - Quality Time: Engage in activities that foster connection and closeness.

  - Vulnerability: Deepen emotional bonds through openness.

- Physical Intimacy:

- Communicating Needs: Discuss physical preferences and desires openly.

- Affectionate Touch: Incorporate daily physical closeness, like hugging and cuddling.

- Exploring Together: Be open to new experiences and communicate boundaries.

- Respecting Boundaries: Ensure mutual comfort and consent in physical interactions.

11.4 Maintaining Boundaries and Respect

- Identifying Boundaries: Understand and communicate your personal limits and needs.

- Clear Communication: Discuss and respect each other's boundaries openly.

- Consistent Respect: Honor boundaries consistently to build and maintain trust.

- Regular Reassessment: Revisit and adjust boundaries as needed to stay relevant.

- Constructive Handling of Violations: Address boundary issues calmly and constructively.

- Balancing Togetherness and Independence: Maintain a healthy mix of shared activities and individual interests.

Summary

Developing trust and intimacy is crucial for a deep and lasting relationship. By understanding the importance of trust, building it over time, nurturing emotional and physical intimacy, and maintaining healthy boundaries, you can create a strong, fulfilling connection with your partner. Implementing these strategies will help ensure a successful and enduring relationship.

Chapter 12: Deepening Connection

Building trust and fostering intimacy are essential for a successful relationship. Trust creates emotional safety, encourages open communication, and establishes reliability. Intimacy deepens both emotional and physical connections. This chapter explores the importance of trust, methods to build it, ways to enhance intimacy, and maintaining boundaries.

12.1 Building Emotional Intimacy

Emotional intimacy is the deep sense of connection and closeness you feel with your partner. It's built on trust, vulnerability, and open communication. Here's how to foster emotional intimacy:

A. Open and Honest Communication

- Transparency: Be truthful about your emotions and thoughts. Sharing your true feelings fosters a deeper connection and understanding.

- Encouragement: Foster a two-way street of open dialogue. Encourage your partner to share their thoughts and feelings openly as well.

B. Active Listening

- Full Attention: Focus entirely on your partner during conversations. Avoid distractions and show that you are fully present.

- Reflecting Back: Paraphrase to show understanding and empathy. Reflecting your partner's words back to them demonstrates that you are listening and validates their feelings.

C. Vulnerability

- Open Up: Share personal and intimate aspects of your life. Being vulnerable allows your partner to see the real you and builds trust.

- Mutual Vulnerability: Encourage your partner to do the same. Create a safe space where both of you can be open and honest without fear of judgment.

D. Emotional Support

- Empathy: Understand and share in your partner's feelings. Show that you genuinely care about their emotional experiences.

- Reassurance: Provide comfort and support consistently. Let your partner know that you are there for them, especially during difficult times.

E. Regular Check-Ins

- Routine Discussions: Set aside time for regular relationship talks. Regular check-ins help maintain a strong connection and address any issues early.

- Proactive Addressing: Tackle issues early to prevent escalation. Addressing concerns proactively prevents misunderstandings and builds trust.

F. Express Appreciation

- Gratitude: Show thankfulness for your partner's actions. Regularly expressing gratitude strengthens your bond and reinforces positive behavior.

- Acknowledgment: Recognize and celebrate their positive traits. Acknowledge the qualities you love about your partner and let them know they are appreciated.

By focusing on these aspects, you can build and maintain deep emotional intimacy with your partner, creating a strong and fulfilling relationship that can withstand the test of time.

12.2 Exploring Physical Intimacy

Physical intimacy is an essential aspect of a romantic relationship. It involves not just sexual activity but also non-sexual touch that fosters closeness. Here's how to explore and deepen physical intimacy:

A. Communication About Physical Needs

- Clear Dialogue: Be open about your physical preferences. Discussing your needs and desires openly helps ensure both partners feel satisfied and understood.

- Comfort Assurance: Ensure mutual comfort and consent. Always make sure that both partners are comfortable and consenting to any physical activity.

B. Affectionate Touch

- Daily Affection: Integrate touch regularly into your interactions. Simple gestures like holding hands, hugging, and cuddling can significantly enhance physical closeness.

- Security Building: Strengthen the sense of physical closeness. Regular affectionate touch helps build a sense of security and connectedness in the relationship.

C. Creating a Comfortable Environment

- Inviting Atmosphere: Make your space warm and comfortable. A cozy and inviting environment can enhance the experience of physical intimacy.

- Relaxation: Create a peaceful environment for intimacy. Reducing stress and distractions helps both partners relax and enjoy their time together.

D. Exploring Together

- Joint Exploration: Try new things together to deepen connection. Exploring new aspects of physical intimacy can keep the relationship exciting and fulfilling.

- Shared Activities: Engage in physical activities that foster closeness. Activities like dancing, exercising together, or even giving each other massages can enhance your physical bond.

E. Respecting Boundaries

- Boundary Respect: Honor each other's limits without question. Respecting boundaries is crucial for ensuring that both partners feel safe and valued.

- Mutual Comfort: Ensure both partners feel safe at all times. Comfort and consent are key components of healthy physical intimacy.

F. Maintaining Regular Intimacy

- Scheduled Intimacy: Plan for regular moments of physical closeness. Scheduling intimate moments ensures that physical connection remains a priority.

- Prioritization: Keep physical connection a consistent priority. Regular physical intimacy helps maintain the bond between partners and strengthens the relationship.

These practices will help you and your partner explore and deepen your physical intimacy, fostering a more satisfying and connected relationship.

12.3 Shared Experiences and Activities

Shared experiences and activities help build a sense of partnership and teamwork. Engaging in activities together strengthens your bond and creates lasting memories. Here's how to incorporate shared experiences into your relationship:

A. Common Interests

- Shared Hobbies: Participate in activities you both love. Engaging in mutual interests fosters deeper connections and enjoyment.

- Camaraderie: Build a stronger partnership through shared fun. Activities you both enjoy can bring you closer and create a sense of camaraderie.

B. Try New Things Together

- Adventurous Spirit: Explore new experiences to strengthen bonds. Trying new activities together keeps the relationship exciting and fresh.

- Memory Building: Create lasting memories through new activities. New experiences often lead to memorable moments you can cherish together.

C. Daily Rituals

- Routine Establishment: Develop consistent, shared rituals. Daily or weekly routines, like morning coffee together, can provide a sense of stability.

- Reliability: Foster a sense of stability through regular activities. Regularly shared activities create a reliable pattern in your relationship.

D. Collaborative Projects

- Joint Projects: Undertake collaborative efforts to build teamwork. Working together on projects, whether home improvements or creative endeavors, strengthens your ability to cooperate.

- Strengthening Bonds: Deepen connection through joint efforts. Collaborative projects can enhance your sense of partnership and mutual achievement.

E. Celebrate Milestones

- Milestone Celebrations: Mark significant events together. Celebrating anniversaries, birthdays, and personal achievements reinforces your bond.

- Bond Reinforcement: Strengthen connection through shared joy. Celebrating milestones together creates a sense of unity and shared history.

F. Supporting Each Other's Passions

- Mutual Support: Encourage and support each other's interests. Showing interest in your partner's hobbies and passions demonstrates care and support.

- Appreciation: Show up for each other's passions and endeavors. Attend each other's events and be enthusiastic about their pursuits.

Incorporating these shared experiences and activities into your relationship will help you build a stronger, more connected partnership.

12.4 Maintaining Individuality within a Relationship

While deepening your connection is essential, maintaining your individuality is equally important. A healthy relationship allows both partners to grow and thrive as individuals. Here's how to balance connection and individuality:

A. Encourage Personal Growth

- Growth Encouragement: Foster individual development. Support each other in pursuing personal interests, hobbies, and skills.

- Pursuit of Goals: Support your partner's personal ambitions. Celebrate their efforts and achievements, and encourage them to reach their goals.

B. Respect Personal Space

- Space Respect: Allow each other time and space to recharge. Understand the need for alone time and respect each other's personal space.

- Well-being: Promote individual well-being through personal time. Encourage activities that contribute to each partner's mental and emotional health.

C. Maintain Friendships

- Friendship Maintenance: Stay connected with personal friends. Maintaining friendships outside of the relationship enriches your social life and provides additional support.

- Support Network: Cultivate a robust social support system. Encourage each other to spend time with friends and family.

D. Balance Togetherness and Independence

- Balanced Time: Manage time together and apart effectively. Ensure you both have opportunities to pursue individual interests while also spending quality time together.

- Individual Pursuits: Encourage each other's independent activities. Support each other in exploring personal passions and hobbies.

E. Celebrate Individual Achievements

- Achievement Recognition: Acknowledge and celebrate successes. Recognize and applaud each other's accomplishments, both big and small.

- Unique Contributions: Value each partner's individual efforts. Appreciate the unique strengths and contributions each person brings to the relationship.

F. Healthy Boundaries

- Boundary Setting: Clearly define personal limits. Establish and respect boundaries to ensure both partners feel comfortable and secure.

- Respect Boundaries: Ensure both partners feel comfortable and respected. Honoring boundaries strengthens trust and mutual respect.

By maintaining individuality within your relationship, you create a healthy balance that allows both partners to grow and thrive. This balance contributes to a stronger, more fulfilling partnership.

Chapter 12 Review: Deepening Connection

Chapter 12 focuses on deepening connections in relationships through emotional and physical intimacy, shared experiences, and maintaining individuality.

12.1 Building Emotional Intimacy

- Open Communication: Share your thoughts and feelings honestly to build trust.

- Active Listening: Give full attention to your partner and reflect back what they say to show understanding.

- Vulnerability: Share your fears, insecurities, and dreams to deepen your emotional bond.

- Emotional Support: Offer empathy, encouragement, and reassurance during tough times.

- Regular Check-Ins: Schedule frequent discussions to address any concerns and keep the lines of communication open.

- Express Appreciation: Regularly acknowledge and appreciate your partner's efforts and qualities to strengthen your bond.

12.2 Exploring Physical Intimacy

- Communication: Discuss your physical needs and desires openly to ensure mutual satisfaction and respect.

- Affectionate Touch: Incorporate touch into daily routines, such as holding hands, hugging, and cuddling, to build closeness and security.

- Comfortable Environment: Create a relaxing, inviting space conducive to physical intimacy.

- Exploring Together: Be open to trying new physical activities and experiences together to enhance your connection.

- Respecting Boundaries: Always honor each other's limits and ensure mutual comfort and safety.

- Regular Intimacy: Prioritize physical closeness, even with busy schedules, to maintain a strong connection.

12.3 Shared Experiences and Activities

- Common Interests: Engage in hobbies and activities you both enjoy to build camaraderie and have fun together.

- Try New Things: Explore new activities and adventures together to create exciting and lasting memories.

- Daily Rituals: Establish consistent shared routines, such as a morning coffee ritual or weekly date night, to foster stability and reliability.

- Collaborative Projects: Work on projects together, like home improvement or gardening, to build teamwork and strengthen your bond.

- Celebrate Milestones: Mark significant achievements and events, like anniversaries or promotions, to reinforce your connection through shared joy.

- Support Each Other: Encourage and attend each other's events and interests to show support and appreciation.

12.4 Maintaining Individuality

- Encourage Growth: Support each other's personal development and goals to foster individual growth and success.

- Respect Space: Allow personal time and space for each partner to recharge and focus on their well-being.

- Maintain Friendships: Keep up with individual social circles and friendships to cultivate a robust support system outside the relationship.

- Balance Togetherness and Independence: Manage time spent together and apart effectively to maintain a healthy balance.

- Celebrate Achievements: Recognize and celebrate each other's individual successes to appreciate and honor unique contributions.

- Healthy Boundaries: Establish and respect personal limits and boundaries to ensure comfort and mutual respect.

Summary

Deepening your connection involves building emotional and physical intimacy, engaging in shared experiences, and maintaining individuality. By following these practical steps, you can create a balanced and fulfilling partnership that ensures a strong and enduring bond.

Chapter 13: Long-Term Relationship Success

Building a successful long-term relationship requires more than just love and passion. It demands consistent effort, mutual respect, and a deep commitment to growth and connection. This chapter explores essential strategies for sustaining love and affection, resolving conflicts effectively, supporting each other's growth, and planning for a shared future. By integrating these practices into your relationship, you can create a lasting and fulfilling partnership.

13.1 Sustaining Love and Affection

Maintaining love and affection in a long-term relationship requires consistent effort and intentional actions. Here's how to sustain love and affection over time:

A. Regular Expressions of Love

- Verbal Affirmations: Regularly tell your partner how much you love and appreciate them. Words of affirmation reinforce emotional bonds.

- Small Gestures: Show love through small acts of kindness and thoughtfulness. Little things like leaving love notes or making their favorite meal can make a big difference.

B. Physical Affection

- Daily Touch: Incorporate physical affection into your daily routine. Simple gestures like holding hands, hugging, and kissing can strengthen your connection.

- Intimate Moments: Ensure regular physical closeness to maintain intimacy. Make time for intimacy and physical connection to keep the spark alive.

C. Quality Time

- Dedicated Time: Schedule regular moments to be together without interruptions. Prioritize your partner by setting aside time just for the two of you.

- Enjoyable Activities: Participate in activities that you both find enjoyable and engaging. Shared experiences can deepen your bond and create lasting memories.

D. Shared Interests

- Common Hobbies: Engage in activities that you both love. Finding common hobbies can bring you closer together and provide ongoing enjoyment.

- Joint Projects: Work on projects or hobbies that bring you closer together. Collaborative efforts can strengthen your partnership and teamwork.

E. Keep the Fun Alive

- Surprises: Plan unexpected fun activities or outings. Spontaneous surprises can keep the relationship exciting and show that you care.

- Adventures: Keep the relationship exciting with new and fun experiences. Trying new things together can invigorate your connection and create shared excitement.

F. Express Gratitude

- Gratitude: Show appreciation for the small and big things they do. Regularly expressing gratitude helps your partner feel valued and loved.

- Acknowledgment: Recognize and value their contributions to the relationship. Acknowledging their efforts fosters mutual respect and appreciation.

By incorporating these practices into your relationship, you can sustain love and affection, ensuring a strong and lasting bond with your partner.

13.2 Effective Conflict Resolution

Conflicts are inevitable in any long-term relationship, but handling them effectively can strengthen your bond. Here's how to resolve conflicts constructively:

A. Stay Calm and Respectful

- Calm Demeanor: Keep your emotions in check during disagreements. Take deep breaths and approach the conversation with a level head.

- Respectful Tone: Use a respectful and kind tone when discussing issues. Avoid yelling, sarcasm, or dismissive language.

B. Listen Actively

- Empathy: Show that you understand and care about their perspective. Acknowledge their feelings and validate their experiences.

- Active Listening: Pay full attention and respond thoughtfully. Avoid interrupting and make sure you fully understand their point before responding.

C. Focus on the Issue, Not the Person

- Issue-Focused: Keep the discussion on the problem, not personal attacks. Address the specific issue at hand without bringing up unrelated past grievances.

- "I" Statements: Express how you feel without blaming your partner. Use statements like "I feel..." rather than "You always..."

D. Seek to Understand

- Common Ground: Identify areas of agreement and build on them. Finding shared values or goals can help in reaching a resolution.

- Compromise: Be willing to find a middle ground that works for both. Flexibility and willingness to adjust your position can lead to a satisfactory outcome.

E. Take Breaks if Needed

- Cooling Off: Take time to calm down before continuing. If emotions run high, agree to take a break and revisit the conversation when both are calmer.

- Scheduled Discussion: Set a specific time to revisit the issue. This shows commitment to resolving the conflict and provides time to reflect.

F. Follow Up

- Check-Ins: Make sure both partners feel the issue is resolved. Follow up to ensure there are no lingering misunderstandings.

- Closure: Ensure there are no lingering feelings of resentment. Address any remaining concerns and reaffirm your commitment to moving forward positively.

By adopting these strategies, you can navigate conflicts effectively, fostering a stronger, more resilient relationship.

13.3 Supporting Each Other's Growth

Supporting each other's personal growth and development is vital for a thriving long-term relationship. Here's how to foster mutual growth:

A. Encourage Individual Goals

- Goal Support: Help each other pursue personal ambitions. Offer assistance and resources to help your partner achieve their goals.

- Encouragement: Motivate and encourage your partner's growth. Provide positive reinforcement and celebrate their efforts.

B. Celebrate Achievements

- Achievement Recognition: Celebrate milestones and successes. Acknowledge and reward your partner's accomplishments, both big and small.

- Pride and Support: Show pride in your partner's accomplishments. Let them know how proud you are of their achievements and the hard work they put in.

C. Provide Emotional Support

- Emotional Encouragement: Be a source of support and comfort. Offer words of encouragement and be there during challenging times.

- Listening Ear: Offer empathy and understanding during tough times. Sometimes, just being there to listen can make a significant difference.

D. Share Growth Experiences

- Joint Growth: Participate in activities that foster mutual growth. Engage in activities such as attending workshops, learning new skills, or setting joint goals.

- New Experiences: Explore new hobbies and interests together. Trying new things can strengthen your bond and provide fresh perspectives.

E. Respect Independence

- Personal Space: Give each other time to pursue individual interests. Respect the need for personal space and allow for individual pursuits.

- Self-Discovery: Encourage personal growth and independence. Support your partner's journey of self-discovery and personal development.

F. Be a Source of Inspiration

- Lead by Example: Show dedication to your own growth. Demonstrate commitment to your personal goals and self-improvement.

- Inspire Growth: Motivate your partner through your actions. Your efforts and achievements can inspire your partner to strive for their own growth.

By fostering an environment of mutual support and encouragement, you can help each other grow and thrive, leading to a more fulfilling and resilient relationship.

13.4 Planning for the Future Together

Planning for the future is essential for building a strong and lasting partnership. Here's how to create a shared vision for the future:

A. Discuss Long-Term Goals

- Open Discussions: Regularly talk about future aspirations. Ensure that both partners are aligned and understand each other's dreams and ambitions.

- Shared Vision: Create a common vision for the future. Work together to outline what you both want to achieve in the long run.

B. Set Joint Goals

- Common Goals: Identify and pursue goals together. Whether it's buying a home, traveling, or starting a family, set goals that you both can work towards.

- Teamwork: Strengthen your bond through shared objectives. Collaborate and support each other in achieving these joint goals.

C. Create a Financial Plan

- Financial Planning: Develop a joint approach to managing money. Discuss your financial priorities and create a plan that suits both partners.

- Budgeting and Saving: Plan for future financial stability. Establish a budget, save for important milestones, and ensure financial security.

D. Plan for Life Changes

- Life Planning: Prepare for significant changes together. Discuss how you will handle major life events such as career changes, moving, or having children.

- Joint Navigation: Work as a team to handle life transitions. Support each other through these changes and adapt as needed.

E. Build a Support Network

- Support System: Develop a network of supportive people. Surround yourselves with friends and family who encourage and support your relationship.

- Encouragement: Seek advice and encouragement from trusted sources. Lean on your support network during challenging times.

F. Revisit and Adjust Plans

- Plan Review: Regularly assess and adjust your plans. Periodically review your goals and progress to ensure they remain relevant and achievable.

- Flexibility: Adapt to changing circumstances together. Be open to modifying your plans as needed to accommodate new situations and opportunities.

By creating a shared vision for the future and working together to achieve it, you can build a solid foundation for a lasting and fulfilling partnership. This collaborative approach ensures that both partners are committed to the relationship's long-term success.

Chapter 13 Review: Long-Term Relationship Success

Chapter 13 explores strategies to achieve long-term relationship success, focusing on sustaining love and affection, resolving conflicts effectively, supporting each other's growth, and planning for a shared future.

13.1 Sustaining Love and Affection

Maintaining love and affection over time requires consistent effort:

- Regular Expressions of Love: Continuously express love and appreciation through words and actions.

- Physical Affection: Regular touch, such as holding hands and hugging, reinforces closeness.

- Quality Time: Spend distraction-free time together engaging in enjoyable activities.

- Shared Interests: Pursue common hobbies to strengthen your connection.

- Keep the Fun Alive: Infuse spontaneity and surprises into the relationship.

- Express Gratitude: Regularly acknowledge and appreciate your partner's contributions.

13.2 Effective Conflict Resolution

Handling conflicts constructively can strengthen your bond:

- Stay Calm and Respectful: Approach conflicts with a composed and respectful attitude.

- Listen Actively: Give full attention, show empathy, and understand your partner's perspective.

- Focus on the Issue, Not the Person: Address the problem without personal attacks using "I" statements.

- Seek to Understand: Find common ground and be open to compromise.

- Take Breaks if Needed: Cool down before continuing heated discussions.

- Follow Up: Ensure the conflict is fully resolved with no lingering resentments.

13.3 Supporting Each Other's Growth

Fostering mutual growth is vital for a thriving relationship:

- Encourage Individual Goals: Support each other's personal ambitions and aspirations.

- Celebrate Achievements: Acknowledge and celebrate each other's successes.

- Provide Emotional Support: Offer empathy and encouragement during challenging times.

- Share Growth Experiences: Engage in activities that promote mutual growth.

- Respect Independence: Allow space and freedom for personal growth and self-discovery.

- Be a Source of Inspiration: Inspire your partner through your own commitment to growth.

13.4 Planning for the Future Together

Creating a shared vision for the future strengthens your partnership:

- Discuss Long-Term Goals: Regularly talk about your future aspirations and dreams.

- Set Joint Goals: Identify and pursue common goals together.

- Create a Financial Plan: Develop a joint approach to managing finances.

- Plan for Life Changes: Anticipate and navigate significant life changes together.

- Build a Support Network: Cultivate a network of supportive family and friends.

- Revisit and Adjust Plans: Regularly reassess and adapt your plans to stay aligned with your shared vision.

Summary

Achieving long-term relationship success involves sustaining love and affection, resolving conflicts constructively, supporting each other's growth, and planning for the future together. By following these practical steps, you can build a strong, fulfilling, and enduring partnership.

Part 5: Advanced Relationship Dynamics

Chapter 14: Navigating Serious Commitments

Navigating serious commitments in a relationship involves significant transitions and milestones that require careful planning, clear communication, and mutual understanding. This chapter provides comprehensive guidance on how to approach these critical aspects of your partnership.

14.1 Moving In Together

Moving in together is a pivotal step in any relationship, marking a new level of intimacy and commitment. Here's how to navigate this important transition:

A. Discuss Expectations

- Household Responsibilities: Divide chores equitably to maintain a balanced living environment. Establish clear agreements on who handles which tasks to ensure fairness and cooperation.

- Personal Space: Respect each other's need for personal space and alone time. Understand that having time apart can be beneficial for both partners.

B. Create a Financial Plan

- Shared Expenses: Agree on how to manage joint expenses to prevent financial stress. Decide on a system for splitting rent, utilities, groceries, and other shared costs.

- Financial Transparency: Be open about your financial situations to build trust. Discuss debts, savings, and spending habits to avoid surprises and foster transparency.

C. Choose the Right Space

- Location: Choose a convenient location for both partners. Consider factors such as proximity to work, family, and friends, as well as neighborhood amenities.

- Affordability: Ensure the living space fits within your combined budget. Look for a place that meets your needs without overstretching your finances.

D. Establish Boundaries

- Privacy: Define personal spaces to ensure each partner has their own area. Even in shared living spaces, having a designated personal space can help maintain individual comfort.

- Social Boundaries: Discuss social activities and how to balance them with time together. Agree on how often you will have guests and how to handle social commitments.

E. Communicate Openly

- Conflict Resolution: Develop a strategy for resolving disputes peacefully. Agree on a method for addressing disagreements, such as setting aside time to talk calmly about issues.

- Regular Check-Ins: Schedule regular conversations to discuss living arrangements and address any concerns. Regularly check in with each other to ensure both partners are happy with the living situation and to make necessary adjustments.

By carefully planning and openly communicating, moving in together can be a positive and enriching step in your relationship, setting the stage for a harmonious and supportive living arrangement.

14.2 Engagement and Marriage

Engagement and marriage signify a deep commitment to each other. Here's how to navigate these significant life events:

A. Discuss Marriage Goals

- Future Planning: Align on long-term goals and aspirations. Make sure you both have a shared vision for your future together.

- Children: Discuss if and when you want children and your parenting philosophies. Understanding each other's views on family planning is crucial.

B. Plan the Proposal

- Personal Touch: Incorporate elements that are significant to your relationship. Make the proposal meaningful by including shared memories or personal symbols.

- Surprise Factor: Ensure the proposal is a pleasant surprise. Plan it in a way that reflects your partner's personality and preferences.

C. Engagement Period

- Future Vision: Plan your life together beyond the wedding day. Discuss your future home, career plans, and life goals.

- Wedding Planning: Collaborate on wedding details to reflect both partners' preferences. Work together to plan a wedding that represents your unique bond.

D. Premarital Counseling

- Communication Skills: Enhance your communication and conflict-resolution skills. Counseling can provide tools to navigate future challenges.

- Future Challenges: Prepare for potential challenges and how to navigate them. Discuss topics such as finances, in-laws, and career changes.

E. Plan the Wedding

- Joint Decisions: Make planning decisions together to avoid stress. Ensure both partners have a say in the wedding plans.

- Budgeting: Agree on a wedding budget and stick to it. Financial planning for the wedding can prevent unnecessary stress and disagreements.

F. Focus on the Marriage

- Long-Term Relationship: Focus on building a sustainable and fulfilling marriage. Prioritize your relationship over the wedding day itself.

- Lifelong Commitment: Strengthen your commitment through shared goals and values. Continue to nurture your relationship with regular check-ins and shared activities.

By approaching engagement and marriage with thoughtful planning and open communication, you can build a strong foundation for a lasting and fulfilling relationship.

14.3 Blending Families and Parenting

Blending families and parenting together can be rewarding but also challenging. Here's how to approach this complex dynamic:

A. Open Communication

- Parenting Styles: Align on parenting approaches to present a united front. Discuss and agree on the values and methods you want to instill in your children.

- Discipline Strategies: Agree on consistent discipline methods. Consistency is key to providing a stable environment for the children.

B. Build Relationships with Stepchildren

- Trust Building: Create trust through patience and understanding. Give stepchildren time to adjust and build trust at their own pace.

- Engagement: Actively engage in the children's activities and interests. Show genuine interest and participation in their lives.

C. Set Clear Roles and Boundaries

- Role Clarity: Clearly define the role of each parent and stepparent. Ensure everyone understands their responsibilities and boundaries.

- Boundary Respect: Respect the established boundaries to maintain harmony. Avoid overstepping roles to prevent conflicts.

D. Create New Family Traditions

- Traditions: Establish regular family activities that everyone enjoys. Create new traditions that foster unity and a sense of belonging.

- Unity: Foster a sense of belonging through shared traditions. These traditions can help blend the family together over time.

E. Seek Support

- Professional Guidance: Seek help from therapists to manage family dynamics. Professional guidance can provide strategies and support for complex situations.

- Support Groups: Join support groups for blended families. Sharing experiences with others in similar situations can be very helpful.

F. Prioritize Couple Time

- Date Nights: Schedule regular date nights or alone time. Maintaining your relationship is crucial for the family's overall well-being.

- Relationship Maintenance: Keep your romantic connection strong. Continue to nurture your relationship amidst the complexities of blended family life.

By implementing these strategies, you can navigate the challenges of blending families and parenting effectively, creating a harmonious and supportive family environment.

14.4 Financial Planning and Shared Goals

Financial planning is a crucial aspect of navigating serious commitments. Here's how to manage your finances and set shared goals:

A. Open Financial Communication

- Financial Honesty: Be transparent about your financial situation. Share information about income, expenses, debts, and financial habits.

- Debt Management: Discuss strategies for managing and reducing debt. Create a plan to pay off existing debts and avoid accumulating new ones.

B. Set Financial Goals

- Joint Goals: Agree on mutual financial goals and work towards them together. This might include saving for a house, a car, or a vacation.

- Future Planning: Plan for significant future expenses and savings. Consider long-term goals such as education for children, buying property, or retirement.

C. Create a Budget

- Budgeting: Create and stick to a budget that works for both partners. Outline monthly income, necessary expenses, and discretionary spending.

- Expense Tracking: Monitor spending to stay on track with financial goals. Use apps or spreadsheets to keep track of your expenditures.

D. Emergency Fund

- Safety Net: Establish an emergency fund for financial security. Aim to save enough to cover three to six months' worth of living expenses.

- Savings Goals: Set specific savings targets for emergencies. Regularly contribute to this fund to build a robust financial cushion.

E. Invest Wisely

- Investment Planning: Make informed investment decisions together. Research and choose investment opportunities that align with your financial goals.

- Retirement Planning: Plan for a comfortable retirement. Contribute to retirement accounts and consider seeking advice from a financial planner.

F. Regular Financial Check-Ins

- Financial Reviews: Regularly review and adjust your financial plans. Schedule periodic meetings to discuss your financial situation and make necessary adjustments.

- Accountability: Ensure mutual accountability in financial decisions. Hold each other responsible for sticking to the budget and working towards shared goals.

By implementing these financial strategies, you can create a stable and prosperous financial future together. Open communication and joint planning will help you achieve your shared financial goals and strengthen your partnership.

Chapter 14 Review: Navigating Serious Commitments

Chapter 14 delves into navigating serious commitments in relationships, providing comprehensive strategies for moving in together, engagement and marriage, blending families and parenting, and financial planning.

14.1 Moving In Together

- Discuss Expectations: Have open conversations about household responsibilities, chores, personal space, and routines to prevent misunderstandings.

- Create a Financial Plan: Decide how to handle expenses such as rent, utilities, and groceries, and whether to split costs equally or proportionally.

- Choose the Right Space: Select a living space that meets both partners' needs in terms of location, size, and affordability.

- Establish Boundaries: Set clear boundaries to respect personal space and privacy, including alone time and workspaces.

- Communicate Openly: Maintain honest communication about feelings and issues to address concerns promptly.

- Plan for Conflict Resolution: Develop strategies for resolving disputes, such as regular check-ins or scheduled discussions.

14.2 Engagement and Marriage

- Discuss Marriage Goals: Before getting engaged, talk about children, career aspirations, and living arrangements to ensure compatibility.

- Plan the Proposal: Consider your partner's preferences and plan a meaningful and memorable proposal.

- Engagement Period: Use this time to strengthen your relationship and plan your future beyond the wedding day.

- Premarital Counseling: Consider counseling to address important topics and prepare for potential challenges.

- Plan the Wedding: Collaborate on wedding planning to reflect both partners' preferences and values, and be prepared to compromise.

- Focus on the Marriage: Prioritize building a strong, loving, and supportive partnership beyond the wedding day.

14.3 Blending Families and Parenting

- Open Communication: Discuss parenting styles, values, and expectations to ensure consistency.

- Build Relationships with Stepchildren: Take time to build trust and positive relationships with each other's children.

- Set Clear Roles and Boundaries: Define parental roles and boundaries to maintain harmony.

- Create New Family Traditions: Develop traditions that include all family members to foster unity and belonging.

- Seek Support: Consider family therapists or support groups to navigate complex emotions and dynamics.

- Prioritize Couple Time: Ensure quality time with your partner to nurture your relationship amidst parenting responsibilities.

14.4 Financial Planning and Shared Goals

- Open Financial Communication: Discuss your financial situations, including income, debts, savings, and spending habits to build trust and prevent conflicts.

- Set Financial Goals: Establish short-term and long-term goals, such as saving for a house, retirement, or travel.

- Create a Budget: Develop a joint budget and track expenses to meet financial goals.

- Emergency Fund: Build an emergency fund to cover unexpected expenses, aiming for three to six months' worth of living expenses.

- Invest Wisely: Discuss investment strategies and plan for retirement, potentially with the help of a financial advisor.

- Regular Financial Check-Ins: Schedule regular reviews to discuss progress, adjust plans, and ensure accountability.

Summary

Navigating serious commitments requires careful planning, open communication, and mutual support. By addressing key areas such as moving in together, engagement and marriage, blending families and parenting, and financial planning, you can build a strong, stable, and fulfilling partnership.

This chapter provides practical, step-by-step guidance to help you navigate these significant milestones with confidence and ease, ensuring a successful and enduring relationship.

Chapter 15: Dealing with External Influences

Navigating external influences is a critical component of maintaining a healthy and robust relationship. This chapter provides comprehensive guidance on managing relationships with in-laws, balancing friendships, handling social media, and coping with life changes and stress. Each section offers practical steps and insights to help you and your partner thrive despite external pressures.

15.1 Managing Relationships with In-Laws

Building and maintaining positive relationships with in-laws can be crucial for a successful partnership. Here's how to manage these relationships effectively:

A. Establish Boundaries

- Household Responsibilities: Decide how often visits are acceptable and how to handle unannounced drop-ins. Clearly communicate these boundaries to avoid misunderstandings.

- Consistency: Maintain these boundaries consistently to prevent misunderstandings. Ensure that both partners agree on and uphold these limits.

B. Show Respect and Appreciation

- Gestures: Simple gestures like sending thank-you notes or remembering birthdays can build goodwill. Small acts of kindness can go a long way in fostering positive relationships.

- Positive Reinforcement: Regularly express appreciation to reinforce positive interactions. Compliment their efforts and show gratitude for their support.

C. Communicate Openly

- Conflict Resolution: Calmly explain your perspective and listen to theirs to resolve misunderstandings. Open and respectful communication can prevent conflicts from escalating.

- Proactive Engagement: Regularly check in with your in-laws to maintain a healthy relationship. Show interest in their lives and keep the lines of communication open.

D. Spend Quality Time Together

- Involvement: Attend family dinners, holiday celebrations, and other special occasions. Being present at family events shows that you value their company and are committed to building a strong relationship.

- Shared Activities: Find common interests to enjoy together, fostering mutual respect and understanding. Activities like cooking, gardening, or sports can create bonding opportunities.

E. Support Your Partner

- Unified Front: Present a united front in family matters to strengthen your partnership. Show your in-laws that you and your partner are a team and support each other's decisions.

- Empathy: Encourage your partner to communicate their feelings and work together to resolve issues. Understanding and supporting each other can help navigate family dynamics more smoothly.

F. Seek Common Ground

- Shared Hobbies: Engage in activities that both you and your in-laws enjoy. Finding common interests can build stronger connections and mutual respect.

- Collaborative Efforts: Work together on projects or tasks to build camaraderie. Collaborating on family events or home improvements can create a sense of teamwork and shared purpose.

By implementing these strategies, you can build and maintain positive relationships with your in-laws, contributing to a more harmonious and supportive family environment.

15.2 Balancing Friends and Your Relationship

Balancing time between friends and your relationship is essential for maintaining a healthy social life and a strong partnership. Here's how to achieve that balance:

A. Communicate Your Needs

- Agreements: Agree on certain times or days for socializing with friends. Establish a schedule that allows for regular interactions with both friends and each other.

- Understanding: Ensure mutual understanding and respect for each other's social needs. Discuss and acknowledge the importance of maintaining individual friendships.

B. Prioritize Quality Time

- Scheduling: Balance your schedule to include activities with friends and dedicated time for your relationship. Make a conscious effort to plan both social outings and intimate moments.

- Engagement: Plan date nights or weekend getaways to nurture your bond with your partner. Quality time together helps maintain a strong emotional connection.

C. Include Your Partner

- Social Integration: Joint activities like group outings or dinner parties can integrate your social circles. This helps both partners feel connected to each other's friends.

- Involvement: Help your partner feel included in your social life to build a supportive network. Invite them to join activities with your friends and participate in theirs.

D. Respect Each Other's Friendships

- Independence: Allow each other the freedom to nurture individual friendships. Recognize the importance of personal space and social interactions outside the relationship.

- Trust: Avoid being overly possessive or controlling to maintain trust. Trust is key in ensuring both partners feel comfortable with their social interactions.

E. Set Boundaries

- Allocation: Decide on certain nights dedicated to friends and others reserved for quality time together. This clear allocation helps manage expectations and prevents conflicts.

- Balance: Ensure a healthy balance to prevent feelings of neglect. Regularly assess and adjust your schedules to maintain harmony.

F. Regular Check-Ins

- Adjustments: Use these discussions to make any necessary adjustments. Regularly evaluate how the balance is working and make changes as needed.

- Reinforcement: Reinforce your commitment to each other. Express appreciation for the efforts made to balance social life and relationship needs.

By effectively managing time with friends and your partner, you can maintain a fulfilling social life while strengthening your relationship. Clear communication, mutual respect, and regular check-ins are key to achieving this balance.

15.3 Handling Social Media and Privacy

Social media can have a significant impact on relationships, and managing it effectively is crucial for maintaining privacy and trust. Here's how to handle social media in your relationship:

A. Discuss Social Media Boundaries

- Guidelines: Agree on the types of posts, photos, and comments that are appropriate. Establish clear guidelines to prevent misunderstandings and conflicts.

- Mutual Respect: Ensure both partners are comfortable with the established boundaries. Respect each other's preferences regarding online presence.

B. Respect Privacy

- Consent: Always ask before posting anything involving your partner. Obtain their consent to ensure they are comfortable with the shared content.

- Sensitivity: Be mindful of their privacy preferences. Avoid sharing personal information or photos that they might consider private.

C. Monitor Interactions

- Transparency: Maintain transparency in your online interactions. Be open about your online activities and interactions with others.

- Respect: Avoid flirting or engaging in inappropriate behaviors online. Uphold the same standards of respect online as you do in person.

D. Limit Social Media Use

- No-Phone Zones: Establish "no phone" zones or times to focus on each other. Designate specific times, such as during meals or date nights, to be free from social media distractions.

- Presence: Ensure undivided attention during meals or before bedtime. Prioritize quality time together without the interference of digital devices.

E. Handle Conflicts Offline

- Private Discussions: Discuss grievances privately to maintain dignity and privacy. Avoid airing personal issues on social media.

- Effective Communication: Use direct and respectful communication to resolve issues. Address conflicts in person or through private channels.

F. Be Transparent

- Account Sharing: Share access to social media accounts if both partners agree. This can enhance trust but should be mutually consensual.

- Privacy Balance: Respect each other's privacy while maintaining transparency. Find a balance that ensures both partners feel secure and respected.

By implementing these strategies, you can navigate the complexities of social media and privacy in your relationship, fostering trust and maintaining a healthy connection. Clear communication and mutual respect are key to successfully managing social media's impact on your partnership.

15.4 Coping with Life Changes and Stress

Life changes and stress can put a strain on relationships, but managing them effectively can strengthen your bond. Here's how to cope with life changes and stress together:

A. Communicate Openly

- Honesty: Regular, honest communication helps both partners feel supported and understood. Sharing your feelings openly can prevent misunderstandings and build trust.

- Active Listening: Listen actively and empathetically to each other's concerns. Show that you value and understand your partner's perspective.

B. Offer Support and Empathy

- Reassurance: Simple acts of kindness and words of encouragement can make a big difference. Providing reassurance during stressful times can help alleviate anxiety.

- Emotional Support: Provide a listening ear and emotional support. Be present for your partner and offer comfort during difficult moments.

C. Develop Coping Strategies

- Healthy Habits: This can include exercise, meditation, hobbies, or seeking professional help. Engaging in healthy activities can reduce stress and improve well-being.

- Routine: Find what works best for both of you and make it a part of your routine. Establishing a consistent routine can create a sense of stability and control.

D. Maintain Routine and Stability

- Grounding Rituals: Regular date nights, morning coffee together, or evening walks can be grounding rituals. These routines provide a sense of normalcy and continuity.

- Consistency: Maintain consistent routines to provide a sense of normalcy. Stability in daily life can help manage stress more effectively.

E. Focus on Teamwork

- Joint Effort: Whether it's financial stress, health issues, or job changes, face them together to strengthen your partnership. Working as a team fosters unity and resilience.

- Problem-Solving: Work together to find and implement solutions. Collaborative problem-solving can lead to more effective and satisfying outcomes.

F. Seek External Support

- Support Systems: Sometimes an outside perspective can provide valuable insights and relief. Friends, family, or support groups can offer additional perspectives and support.

- Professional Help: Support groups or counseling can offer additional tools and strategies. Professional guidance can help navigate particularly challenging situations.

By implementing these strategies, you can effectively manage life changes and stress together, reinforcing your relationship and enhancing your ability to cope with future challenges. Clear communication, mutual support, and proactive coping mechanisms are key to maintaining a strong and resilient partnership.

Chapter 15 Review: Dealing with External Influences

Chapter 15 delves into managing external influences in relationships, providing strategies for maintaining a healthy partnership despite external pressures. It covers managing relationships with in-laws, balancing friendships, handling social media, and coping with life changes and stress.

15.1 Managing Relationships with In-Laws

- Establish Boundaries: Clearly define and maintain boundaries to ensure mutual respect and comfort.

- Show Respect and Appreciation: Acknowledge your in-laws' role and express gratitude regularly.

- Communicate Openly: Address issues directly and respectfully to prevent misunderstandings.

- Spend Quality Time Together: Participate in family gatherings and traditions to strengthen bonds.

- Support Your Partner: Stand by your partner and present a united front in family matters.

- Seek Common Ground: Find shared interests or activities to build camaraderie.

15.2 Balancing Friends and Your Relationship

- Communicate Your Needs: Discuss the importance of maintaining friendships and social time.

- Prioritize Quality Time: Balance time spent with friends and your partner to nurture both relationships.

- Include Your Partner: Integrate your partner into social gatherings when appropriate.

- Respect Each Other's Friendships: Encourage and respect each other's social connections.

- Set Boundaries: Establish and adhere to boundaries regarding social time.

- Regular Check-Ins: Have discussions to ensure satisfaction with the balance between social life and relationship time.

15.3 Handling Social Media and Privacy

- Discuss Social Media Boundaries: Set clear guidelines on what to share about your relationship online.

- Respect Privacy: Avoid posting private or sensitive information without consent.

- Monitor Interactions: Be mindful of online behaviors to prevent jealousy or mistrust.

- Limit Social Media Use: Establish "no-phone" times to focus on each other.

- Handle Conflicts Offline: Address social media-related issues privately.

- Be Transparent: Maintain openness about social media activities while respecting privacy.

15.4 Coping with Life Changes and Stress

- Communicate Openly: Share feelings and concerns honestly during stressful times.

- Offer Support and Empathy: Validate your partner's feelings and provide reassurance.

- Develop Coping Strategies: Create routines and strategies to manage stress together.

- Maintain Routine and Stability: Keep consistent routines to provide a sense of normalcy.

- Focus on Teamwork: Approach challenges collaboratively to strengthen your bond.

- Seek External Support: Don't hesitate to seek help from friends, family, or professionals.

Summary

Dealing with external influences requires effective communication, mutual respect, and proactive strategies. By managing relationships with in-laws, balancing time with friends, handling social media and privacy issues, and coping with life changes and stress, you can protect and strengthen your partnership. This chapter provides practical guidance to navigate these external influences successfully, ensuring a resilient and enduring relationship.

Chapter 16: Specific Relationship Types

Navigating specific types of relationships requires tailored strategies and an understanding of unique challenges. This chapter provides comprehensive guidance for long-distance relationships, intercultural and interfaith relationships, and relationships under different life circumstances.

16.1 Long-Distance Relationships

Long-distance relationships present unique challenges but can also be deeply rewarding. Here's how to navigate them successfully:

A. Building Trust and Communication

- Prioritize Communication: Set regular times to talk and stick to them. Use various forms of communication like video calls, phone calls, texting, and emails to stay connected. Consistency helps maintain the connection.

- Be Honest and Transparent: Share your feelings, daily experiences, and any concerns openly. Honesty builds trust and prevents misunderstandings. Regular updates about your day-to-day life can bridge the physical gap.

- Set Expectations: Discuss and set clear expectations regarding communication frequency, visits, and relationship goals. Having shared goals and understanding each other's expectations helps in avoiding disappointments.

- Use Technology Wisely: Leverage technology to bridge the distance. Use apps and tools that facilitate communication and make staying in touch easier, such as shared calendars, countdown apps for visits, and video call platforms.

B. Creative Ways to Stay Connected

- Virtual Dates: Plan virtual dates like watching a movie together online, playing online games, or cooking the same meal while video chatting. These shared activities create a sense of togetherness.

- Send Care Packages: Surprise each other with thoughtful gifts or care packages filled with personal items, favorite snacks, and handwritten notes. These tangible items can provide comfort and remind you of each other.

- Share Daily Moments: Share photos, videos, and voice messages of your daily activities to make each other feel included in your lives. This keeps you updated on each other's lives and reinforces your bond.

- Collaborate on Projects: Work on a joint project or hobby that you both enjoy, such as starting a blog, creating art, or learning a new skill together. This shared goal can provide a sense of unity and purpose.

C. Planning Visits and Future Moves

- Regular Visits: Schedule regular visits to spend quality time together. Plan these visits in advance to have something to look forward to. Regular visits help maintain intimacy and provide opportunities for bonding.

- Maximize Time Together: Make the most of your time together by planning meaningful activities and creating lasting memories. Use your time wisely to reinforce your connection and enjoy each other's company.

- Discuss Future Plans: Have open conversations about your long-term plans and goals, including the possibility of moving closer or living together in the future. Planning your future together can give your relationship direction and purpose.

- Financial Planning: Budget for travel expenses and future moves. Ensure both partners contribute to the planning and financial aspects of visits. Financial planning helps avoid stress and ensures that visits and potential moves are feasible.

D. *Overcoming Unique Challenges*

- Time Zone Differences: Be mindful of time zone differences and find suitable times for both partners to communicate. Flexibility and understanding are key to managing time differences.

- Dealing with Loneliness: Acknowledge feelings of loneliness and find ways to cope, such as staying busy with hobbies, spending time with friends, and practicing self-care. It's important to maintain a fulfilling life independently.

- Handling Jealousy and Insecurity: Communicate openly about any feelings of jealousy or insecurity. Reassure each other and work on building trust. Transparency and regular reassurance can help alleviate insecurities.

- Staying Positive: Focus on the positives of your relationship and the future you're building together. Maintain a positive outlook despite the challenges. Remembering why you're committed to each other can help maintain a hopeful perspective.

By implementing these strategies, you can navigate the complexities of a long-distance relationship, maintain a strong connection, and build a future together.

16.2 Intercultural and Interfaith Relationships

Intercultural and interfaith relationships can be incredibly enriching but also require understanding and respect. Here's how to navigate these relationships:

A. *Navigating Cultural Differences*

- Educate Yourself: Learn about your partner's culture, traditions, and customs. Show genuine interest and respect for their background. Understanding your partner's culture fosters respect and appreciation.

- Open Communication: Discuss cultural differences openly and honestly. Address any misunderstandings or misconceptions. Honest conversations help clear up any cultural misunderstandings.

- Celebrate Diversity: Embrace the diversity in your relationship. Celebrate each other's cultural festivals, traditions, and practices. This celebration can enrich your relationship and create new shared experiences.

B. Respecting and Understanding Beliefs

- Discuss Beliefs and Values: Have open conversations about your religious or spiritual beliefs and values. Understand each other's perspectives and find common ground. Mutual respect for each other's beliefs is crucial.

- Respect Each Other's Practices: Respect and support each other's religious practices and rituals. Avoid imposing your beliefs on your partner. Supporting each other's practices builds mutual respect.

- Find Shared Practices: Identify shared practices or values that you both can embrace. This helps build a sense of unity despite differences. Shared values and practices can strengthen your bond.

C. Blending Traditions and Practices

- Create New Traditions: Blend your cultural and religious traditions to create new ones that are meaningful to both of you. This can create a unique shared culture within your relationship.

- Compromise and Adapt: Be willing to compromise and adapt to each other's traditions. Find ways to incorporate both cultures into your life together. Flexibility and adaptation are key to harmony.

- Celebrate Differences: Use your differences as an opportunity to learn and grow. Celebrate the unique aspects of each culture and what they bring to your relationship. This celebration fosters mutual respect and understanding.

D. Communicating with Family and Friends

- Introduce Gradually: Introduce your partner to your family and friends gradually. Give them time to adjust and understand your relationship. Gradual introductions can ease the transition.

- Address Concerns: Be prepared to address any concerns or questions from family and friends about your intercultural or interfaith relationship. Open dialogue can help address and alleviate concerns.

- Seek Support: Find support from friends, mentors, or support groups who understand and appreciate the dynamics of intercultural and interfaith relationships. Support systems can provide valuable advice and encouragement.

Navigating intercultural and interfaith relationships involves mutual respect, open communication, and a willingness to celebrate and blend different traditions and practices. By embracing your differences and finding common ground, you can build a strong, enriching, and harmonious relationship.

16.3 Relationships with Different Life Circumstances

Relationships can be influenced by various life circumstances. Here's how to navigate relationships under different conditions:

A. Dating After Divorce or Loss

- Allow Time for Healing: Ensure you've allowed yourself time to heal from your previous relationship or loss before entering a new one. Emotional readiness is crucial for a healthy new relationship.

- Be Honest About Your Past: Communicate openly about your past experiences and any lingering emotions or challenges. Honesty helps build a foundation of trust.

- Seek Support: Consider counseling or support groups to help navigate the complexities of dating after divorce or loss. Professional support can provide guidance and healing.

- Take It Slow: Move at a pace that feels comfortable for both partners. Avoid rushing into a new relationship. Patience and caution are important for building a solid foundation.

B. Dating with Children

- Communicate Openly: Discuss your children and parenting responsibilities openly with your partner. Ensure they understand and respect your role as a parent. Clear communication helps set realistic expectations.

- Introduce Gradually: Introduce your partner to your children gradually. Allow time for your children to adjust and build a relationship with your partner. Gradual introductions can help ease the transition.

- Set Boundaries: Establish boundaries regarding your children's involvement in the relationship. Prioritize your children's well-being and comfort. Clear boundaries help protect your children's emotional security.

- Involve Your Partner: Involve your partner in family activities and routines to help them integrate into your family life. Inclusion fosters bonding and a sense of belonging.

C. Dating in Different Age Groups (Teenage, 30s, Seniors)

- Understand Different Life Stages: Recognize that different age groups have different life stages and priorities. Be mindful of these differences and communicate openly about them. Awareness of life stages helps in understanding each other's perspectives.

- Common Interests and Goals: Focus on shared interests and goals that can bridge the gap between different age groups. Shared activities and goals can strengthen your connection.

- Respect Individual Experiences: Respect the unique experiences and perspectives that come with different ages. Learn from each other and grow together. Valuing each other's experiences fosters mutual respect.

- Seek Support: If age differences pose challenges, consider seeking advice or counseling to navigate any issues. Professional guidance can provide strategies for overcoming age-related challenges.

D. Managing Health and Wellness in Relationships

- Support Each Other's Health: Encourage and support each other's physical and mental health. This includes maintaining a healthy lifestyle and seeking medical care when needed. Mutual support promotes overall well-being.

- Communicate About Health Issues: Discuss any health issues openly and honestly. Support each other through health challenges and treatments. Transparency about health fosters trust and empathy.

- Healthy Lifestyle Choices: Make healthy lifestyle choices together, such as exercising, eating nutritious foods, and managing stress. Shared healthy habits can strengthen your relationship.

- Mental Health Support: Prioritize mental health by seeking therapy, practicing mindfulness, and supporting each other's emotional well-being. Mental health support is crucial for a balanced and healthy relationship.

Navigating specific relationship types requires understanding, flexibility, and open communication. By addressing the unique challenges posed by different life circumstances, you can build a strong and fulfilling partnership.

Chapter 16 Review: Specific Relationship Types

Navigating different types of relationships requires tailored strategies and understanding. This chapter provides comprehensive guidance for long-distance relationships, intercultural and interfaith relationships, and relationships under various life circumstances.

16.1 Long-Distance Relationships

Long-distance relationships present unique challenges but can be rewarding. Here's how to manage them effectively:

- Building Trust and Communication: Prioritize communication, be honest and transparent, set expectations, and use technology wisely.

- Creative Ways to Stay Connected: Engage in virtual dates, send care packages, share daily moments, and collaborate on projects.

- Planning Visits and Future Moves: Schedule regular visits, maximize time together, discuss future plans, and plan financially.

- Overcoming Unique Challenges: Find suitable times despite time zone differences, manage loneliness, handle jealousy and insecurity, and stay positive.

16.2 Intercultural and Interfaith Relationships

Intercultural and interfaith relationships can be enriching but require understanding and respect.

- Navigating Cultural Differences: Educate yourself about your partner's culture, discuss cultural differences openly, and celebrate diversity.

- Respecting and Understanding Beliefs: Discuss beliefs and values, respect each other's practices, and find shared practices.

- Blending Traditions and Practices: Create new traditions, compromise and adapt, and celebrate differences.

- Communicating with Family and Friends: Introduce family and friends gradually, address their concerns, and seek support.

16.3 Relationships with Different Life Circumstances

Relationships are influenced by various life circumstances. Here's how to navigate them:

- Dating After Divorce or Loss: Allow time for healing, be honest about your past, seek support, and take it slow.

- Dating with Children: Communicate openly about children and parenting roles, introduce your partner gradually, set boundaries, and involve your partner in family activities.

- Dating in Different Age Groups: Understand different life stages, focus on common interests and goals, respect individual experiences, and seek support if needed.

- Managing Health and Wellness in Relationships: Support each other's health, communicate about health issues, make healthy lifestyle choices, and prioritize mental health care.

Summary

Navigating specific relationship types requires understanding, flexibility, and open communication. Whether in a long-distance, intercultural, or interfaith relationship, or dealing with unique life circumstances, these strategies help build a strong and fulfilling partnership. This chapter offers practical guidance for success and happiness in your relationship.

Part 6: Enhancing and Sustaining Relationships

Chapter 17: Keeping the Spark Alive

Maintaining the excitement and passion in a relationship requires ongoing effort, creativity, and dedication. This chapter offers comprehensive strategies to help keep the spark alive and ensure your relationship remains vibrant, fulfilling, and enduring.

17.1 Planning Date Nights and Getaways

Regular date nights and occasional getaways are essential for maintaining intimacy and connection. Here's how to make them special:

A. Set a Schedule

- Designate Regular Nights: Establish a weekly or monthly date night. Consistency helps prioritize your relationship amidst busy schedules.

- Mark Your Calendar: Schedule these dates to ensure they are non-negotiable, creating anticipation and excitement.

B. Be Creative

- Vary Activities: Explore different types of restaurants, attend concerts or events, or take a cooking class together.

- Think Outside the Box: Plan unique activities like stargazing, visiting museums, or participating in workshops to create memorable experiences.

C. Plan Mini Getaways

- Short Trips: Organize weekend getaways to break the routine and create new memories.

- Explore Nearby: Visit nearby towns, nature spots, or book a cozy cabin for a relaxing retreat.

D. Unplug and Focus

- Digital Detox: During date nights and getaways, unplug from digital distractions to focus on each other.

- Be Present: Set aside specific times to check devices, ensuring that the majority of your time together is quality time.

E. Plan Together

- Collaborative Planning: Work as a team to plan dates and trips, ensuring both partners' interests and preferences are considered.

- Mutual Preferences: Discuss and incorporate activities that you both enjoy, fostering teamwork and mutual respect.

By consistently setting aside time for date nights and getaways, being creative with activities, and planning together, you can maintain and strengthen the intimacy and connection in your relationship.

17.2 Exploring New Activities Together

Engaging in new activities together can bring excitement and strengthen your bond. Here's how to discover and enjoy new experiences:

A. Try New Hobbies

- Discover Together: Explore new hobbies like hiking, painting, dancing, or cooking. Finding common interests can enrich your time together.

- Experiment: Be open to each other's interests and find shared activities. This openness can lead to discovering mutual passions.

B. Take Classes Together

- Enroll in Classes: Join workshops or classes such as pottery, photography, or a foreign language. These activities offer structured learning and fun.

- Shared Learning: Learning together fosters teamwork and mutual support, enhancing your connection.

C. Attend Events

- Local Events: Explore concerts, festivals, or theater performances in your area. These events provide opportunities to enjoy cultural and entertainment experiences.

- Shared Experiences: Create lasting memories and fresh conversation topics, enriching your relationship.

D. Travel and Explore

- Day Trips: Travel to new destinations, even for a day. Exploring new places together can be invigorating and fun.

- Bucket List: Make a list of places to visit and start checking them off. Working through a shared list strengthens your bond and gives you goals to achieve together.

E. Challenge Each Other

- Friendly Competitions: Engage in board games, sports, or fitness goals. These activities can be fun and promote healthy competition.

- Motivation: Friendly competition encourages growth and improvement, fostering a supportive environment for both partners.

By trying new hobbies, taking classes together, attending events, traveling, and challenging each other, you can keep your relationship dynamic and engaging. These shared activities not only provide enjoyment but also help you grow closer as a couple.

17.3 Keeping Romance and Passion Alive

Maintaining romance and passion requires ongoing effort and attention. Here's how to keep the flames burning:

A. Express Affection Daily

- Physical Touch: Show affection through small gestures like holding hands, hugging, and kissing. Regular physical touch reinforces your emotional bond.

- Simple Acts: Acknowledge the power of a simple touch or affectionate glance. These small gestures can convey love and appreciation.

B. Leave Love Notes

- Surprise Notes: Leave love notes in unexpected places like bags, cars, or pillows. These little surprises can brighten your partner's day and keep the romance alive.

- Personal Touch: Handwritten notes add a personal, thoughtful element. They show effort and consideration, making your partner feel cherished.

C. Plan Romantic Surprises

- Candlelit Dinners: Plan romantic dinners, surprise dates, or heartfelt gifts. Special, planned moments can create lasting memories and rekindle passion.

- Mystery and Excitement: Keep an element of mystery with periodic surprises. This unpredictability adds excitement and keeps the relationship dynamic.

D. Compliment and Appreciate

- Regular Compliments: Compliment and express appreciation for your partner regularly. Acknowledge their efforts and qualities to make them feel valued.

- Genuine Gratitude: Make it a habit to acknowledge contributions and express gratitude. Sincere appreciation fosters a positive and loving atmosphere.

E. Create Intimate Moments

- Distraction-Free Time: Set aside time for intimate moments without distractions. Focus solely on each other to deepen your connection.

- Regular Routine: Make intimate moments a regular part of your routine. Consistency helps maintain closeness and affection.

F. Maintain Physical Intimacy

- Open Communication: Discuss desires and needs openly. Honest conversations about physical intimacy can enhance your connection.

- Explore Together: Be open to new experiences and maintaining a healthy physical relationship. Exploration keeps the physical aspect of your relationship vibrant and fulfilling.

By expressing affection daily, leaving love notes, planning romantic surprises, complimenting and appreciating each other, creating intimate moments, and maintaining physical intimacy, you can keep romance and passion alive in your relationship. These efforts will help you sustain a loving and passionate connection over the long term.

17.4 Surprising Each Other

Surprises add excitement and spontaneity to a relationship. Here's how to keep the element of surprise alive:

A. Plan Thoughtful Surprises

- Personal Preferences: Plan surprises that reflect your partner's likes and interests. This shows you've been attentive and care about their preferences.

- Thoughtfulness: Show you pay attention to the little things. Even small gestures can have a big impact when they're thoughtful and personalized.

B. Celebrate Small Wins

- Acknowledge Achievements: Celebrate small achievements or milestones. Recognizing these moments can boost your partner's confidence and happiness.

- Positive Reinforcement: Reinforce positive behavior with small celebrations. This encourages a supportive and uplifting environment in your relationship.

C. Spontaneous Adventures

- Unplanned Outings: Plan spontaneous outings like picnics or road trips. These adventures can break the routine and add excitement to your relationship.

- Keep a List: Maintain a list of spontaneous ideas for unexpected moments. Having a list ready ensures you're always prepared to inject some spontaneity.

D. Unexpected Gifts

- Thoughtful Tokens: Give small, meaningful gifts that show you're thinking of your partner. The value lies in the thought, not the price.

- Personal Touch: Focus on thoughtfulness rather than expense. Personalized gifts demonstrate your effort and care.

E. Special Occasions

- Personalize Celebrations: Make special occasions extra special with unique surprises. Tailor the celebration to your partner's tastes and preferences.

- Memorable Events: Plan something unforgettable for birthdays, anniversaries, or just because. Creating lasting memories strengthens your bond.

By planning thoughtful surprises, celebrating small wins, embarking on spontaneous adventures, giving unexpected gifts, and personalizing special occasions, you can keep the excitement and spontaneity alive in your relationship. These efforts show your partner that you care and are invested in maintaining a vibrant and dynamic connection.

17.5 Communicating Openly and Honestly

Open and honest communication is the foundation of a healthy and enduring relationship. Here's how to foster it:

A. Regular Check-Ins

- Scheduled Discussions: Have regular check-ins to discuss your relationship, feelings, and concerns. These conversations help maintain transparency and keep both partners on the same page.

- Prevent Misunderstandings: Ensure both partners feel heard and valued. Regular check-ins can prevent small issues from escalating into larger conflicts.

B. Active Listening

- Full Attention: Give your full attention, acknowledge feelings, and respond thoughtfully. This shows respect and appreciation for your partner's thoughts and emotions.

- Build Trust: Active listening fosters a deeper emotional connection and trust. It demonstrates that you value your partner's perspective and are invested in their well-being.

C. Express Yourself Clearly

- Clear Communication: Communicate needs, desires, and boundaries clearly and respectfully. Clarity in communication reduces misunderstandings and enhances mutual understanding.

- Prevent Conflicts: Use "I" statements to express feelings without sounding accusatory. For example, "I feel upset when..." instead of "You make me upset when..."

D. Handle Conflicts Constructively

- Problem-Solving Mindset: Approach conflicts with a focus on finding solutions. Rather than blaming each other, work together to resolve issues.

- Constructive Resolution: Strengthen your relationship by working through challenges together. Effective conflict resolution can enhance understanding and closeness.

E. Show Empathy and Understanding

- Validate Feelings: Try to understand your partner's perspective and validate their feelings. Acknowledge their emotions even if you don't fully agree with them.

- Mutual Support: Foster mutual respect and support through empathy. Showing that you care about your partner's feelings builds a stronger, more resilient relationship.

By incorporating regular check-ins, practicing active listening, expressing yourself clearly, handling conflicts constructively, and showing empathy and understanding, you can foster open and honest communication in your relationship. This approach not only resolves issues but also builds a deeper, more trusting connection between partners.

17.6 Building and Maintaining Trust

Trust is the cornerstone of any healthy relationship. Here's how to build and maintain it effectively:

A. Be Reliable and Consistent

- Follow through: Ensure you keep promises and commitments to demonstrate dependability.

- Build reliability: Consistently show that your actions align with your words, reinforcing trust over time.

B. Honesty is Key

- Always be honest: Practice honesty, even when it's challenging, to foster a genuine connection.

- Prevent misunderstandings: Promote transparency in all interactions to avoid confusion and build a solid foundation of trust.

C. Embrace Transparency

- Open actions: Be open about your actions, feelings, and intentions to create a trustworthy environment.

- Foster trust: Openness helps prevent misunderstandings and strengthens the trust between partners.

D. Practice Forgiveness and Move Forward

- Let go of grievances: Practice forgiveness to release past grievances and maintain a healthy relationship.

- Focus on healing: Resolve issues constructively and move forward with a positive outlook, reinforcing mutual trust.

E. Support Each Other

- Offer understanding: Provide support and understanding, especially during difficult times, to show you care.

- Strengthen commitment: Regularly offer help and encouragement, strengthening your commitment and trust in each other.

By incorporating these principles, you can create a robust and trustworthy relationship. Each step contributes to a stronger bond, ensuring long-lasting and meaningful connections.

17.7 Growing Together

Personal and relationship growth are essential for a fulfilling partnership. Here's how to grow together:

A. Set Shared Goals

- Common Objectives: Establish and pursue shared goals such as financial plans, travel destinations, or personal development milestones.

- Teamwork: Stay aligned and focused on achieving your future together, reinforcing your bond through mutual efforts.

B. Encourage Personal Growth

- Support New Interests: Actively encourage each other's new interests and skills, fostering an environment of continuous learning.

- Celebrate Achievements: Acknowledge and celebrate each other's progress and accomplishments, no matter how small.

C. Reflect and Adapt

- Regular Reflection: Regularly reflect on your relationship's dynamics and be willing to adapt to changing needs and circumstances.

- Flexibility: Maintain flexibility by discussing areas for improvement and being open to making necessary changes for the betterment of your partnership.

D. Celebrate Growth

- Mark Milestones: Commemorate significant achievements and milestones together, creating lasting memories.

- Recognize Progress: Plan special celebrations to acknowledge and appreciate the progress you've made as a couple.

E. Stay Curious

- Maintain Curiosity: Continue to explore and learn new things about each other, keeping the relationship fresh and engaging.

- Evolving Interests: Show genuine interest in each other's evolving passions and experiences, supporting their personal journeys.

By incorporating these practices, you can foster a relationship that continually grows and adapts, ensuring lasting fulfillment and mutual satisfaction.

Chapter 17 Review: Keeping the Spark Alive

This chapter provides comprehensive strategies for maintaining excitement and passion in a relationship, ensuring it remains vibrant and fulfilling.

17.1 Planning Date Nights and Getaways

- Set a Schedule: Designate regular nights for date nights to prioritize your relationship amidst busy schedules.

- Be Creative: Vary activities to keep things fresh and exciting, such as trying different restaurants, attending events, or taking a cooking class together.

- Plan Mini Getaways: Schedule short trips or weekend retreats to create new memories and break the routine.

- Unplug and Focus: Disconnect from digital distractions during date nights and getaways to fully engage with each other.

- Plan Together: Collaborate on planning to ensure both partners' interests and preferences are considered, fostering teamwork and mutual respect.

17.2 Exploring New Activities Together

- Try New Hobbies: Discover and share new hobbies or activities like hiking, painting, dancing, or cooking.

- Take Classes Together: Enroll in classes or workshops to learn something new together, such as pottery or photography.

- Attend Events: Explore local concerts, festivals, or theater performances to create lasting memories and fresh conversation topics.

- Travel and Explore: Visit new destinations, even if it's just a day trip, to foster a sense of adventure and discovery.

- Challenge Each Other: Engage in friendly competitions or challenges, such as board games, sports, or fitness goals, to add fun and motivation to your relationship.

17.3 Keeping Romance and Passion Alive

- Express Affection Daily: Show physical affection through small gestures like holding hands, hugging, and kissing to maintain closeness.

- Leave Love Notes: Surprise your partner with thoughtful messages in unexpected places like their bag or car.

- Plan Romantic Surprises: Organize special gestures such as candlelit dinners, surprise dates, or heartfelt gifts to show you care.

- Compliment and Appreciate: Regularly express appreciation and admiration for your partner to make them feel valued.

- Create Intimate Moments: Set aside time for distraction-free intimate moments to reinforce your emotional connection.

- Maintain Physical Intimacy: Prioritize physical closeness and communicate openly about desires and needs.

17.4 Surprising Each Other

- Plan Thoughtful Surprises: Tailor surprises to your partner's preferences to show you pay attention to the little things.

- Celebrate Small Wins: Acknowledge and celebrate minor achievements or milestones to show support and pride.

- Spontaneous Adventures: Organize impromptu outings or activities to add spontaneity and excitement.

- Unexpected Gifts: Give thoughtful, unexpected gifts to remind your partner that they are loved and appreciated.

- Special Occasions: Make special occasions memorable with personalized surprises to create lasting memories.

17.5 Communicating Openly and Honestly

- Regular Check-Ins: Schedule regular discussions about your relationship, feelings, and any concerns to ensure both partners feel heard.

- Active Listening: Practice active listening by giving your full attention, acknowledging feelings, and responding thoughtfully.

- Express Yourself Clearly: Communicate needs, desires, and boundaries respectfully to prevent misunderstandings.

- Handle Conflicts Constructively: Approach conflicts with a problem-solving mindset and focus on finding solutions that satisfy both partners.

- Show Empathy and Understanding: Understand and validate your partner's perspective to foster mutual respect and support.

17.6 Building and Maintaining Trust

- Be Reliable and Consistent: Follow through on promises and commitments to build reliability and trust.

- Honesty is Key: Always be truthful, even when it's difficult, to build a foundation of trust.

- Transparency: Be open about your actions, feelings, and intentions to prevent misunderstandings.

- Forgive and Move Forward: Practice forgiveness and let go of past grievances to maintain trust and intimacy.

- Support Each Other: Be supportive and understanding, especially during tough times, to strengthen your bond.

17.7 Growing Together

- Set Shared Goals: Work towards common goals as a couple to stay aligned and focused on your future together.

- Encourage Personal Growth: Support each other's individual development by encouraging new interests and experiences.

- Reflect and Adapt: Regularly reflect on your relationship and be willing to adapt and make changes as needed.

- Celebrate Growth: Acknowledge and celebrate achievements and milestones together to reinforce your bond.

- Stay Curious: Continue to learn and discover new things about your partner to keep your relationship dynamic and exciting.

Summary

To keep the spark alive, invest in regular date nights, exploring new activities, maintaining romance, surprising each other, communicating openly, building trust, and growing together. This chapter offers practical guidance for a vibrant, exciting, and deeply fulfilling relationship. By continually nurturing your bond, you create a strong foundation for lasting love and happiness.

Chapter 18: Personal Growth and Relationship Development

Personal growth and relationship development are closely linked, requiring mutual support, continuous learning, adaptability, and celebration. This chapter provides detailed strategies to help you and your partner grow individually and together, ensuring a successful and enduring relationship.

18.1 Encouraging Each Other's Dreams

Supporting and encouraging each other's dreams is crucial for personal growth and relationship development. Here's how to effectively encourage your partner's aspirations:

A. Show Genuine Interest

- Ask Thoughtful Questions: Engage in meaningful conversations about your partner's goals and passions to show you care.

- Listen Attentively: Give your undivided attention, demonstrate curiosity, and validate their feelings and ideas.

B. Provide Emotional Support

- Offer Affirmation: Use sincere words of encouragement and praise to boost their confidence.

- Be Present: Stand by them during challenging times, offering empathy and a reassuring presence.

C. Celebrate Small Wins

- Acknowledge Achievements: Recognize and celebrate every milestone, no matter how small, to keep motivation high.

- Personal Gestures: Celebrate their successes with thoughtful notes, special dinners, or small gifts to show appreciation.

D. Help Set Goals

- Break Down Dreams: Assist in transforming larger dreams into realistic, manageable goals with clear steps.

- Develop Plans: Collaborate on creating a detailed plan and provide ongoing support and accountability.

E. Offer Practical Help

- Provide Resources: Help by researching, networking, or finding necessary resources to advance their goals.

- Active Involvement: Show commitment to their success through tangible actions and continuous support.

F. Be Patient and Understanding

- Show Compassion: Understand and empathize with setbacks, offering a compassionate ear and encouragement.

- Encourage Resilience: Remind them that setbacks are natural and part of the journey, encouraging perseverance and resilience.

By incorporating these strategies, you can create a nurturing environment where both partners feel empowered and motivated to pursue their dreams, thereby strengthening your bond and fostering mutual growth and fulfillment.

18.2 Continuing Education and Learning Together

Continuing education and learning new things together can strengthen your bond and promote mutual growth. Here's how to incorporate learning into your relationship:

A. Take Classes Together

- Enroll Together: Join classes or workshops that interest both of you to create shared experiences.

- Shared Learning: Enjoy the enrichment and fun of discovering new subjects and skills together.

B. Read and Discuss Books

- Book Club: Start a mini book club for just the two of you, selecting books that spark mutual interest.

- Stimulate Conversations: Engage in thoughtful discussions about the books to deepen your understanding of each other's perspectives.

C. Attend Seminars and Webinars

- Participate Together: Attend seminars or webinars that align with your mutual interests to expand your knowledge base.

- Broaden Knowledge: Keep engaged with shared learning experiences that can inspire and inform your relationship.

D. Explore Online Courses

- Use Platforms: Enroll in online courses together for convenience and flexibility.

- Learn at Your Own Pace: Take advantage of the ability to learn in a comfortable setting and at a pace that suits both of you.

E. Share Knowledge

- Teach Each Other: Share your unique skills and expertise with one another.

- Strengthen Bond: Promote continuous learning and mutual growth by teaching and learning from each other.

F. Set Learning Goals

- Establish Goals: Create shared learning objectives to give your educational pursuits direction and purpose.

- Track Progress: Monitor your progress and celebrate achievements to maintain motivation and a sense of accomplishment.

By embracing these practices, you can create a dynamic and intellectually stimulating relationship that fosters growth, understanding, and a deeper connection.

18.3 Supporting Each Other Through Changes

Life is full of changes, and supporting each other through these transitions is essential for a strong relationship. Here's how to provide support during times of change:

A. Open Communication

- Discuss Changes: Engage in honest and open conversations about upcoming changes and their potential impacts.

- Understand Concerns: Listen actively to each other's worries and expectations, ensuring you address all concerns.

B. Be a Source of Stability

- Reassure: Provide comfort and reassurance to help ease stress and anxiety.

- Reliable Presence: Be a dependable anchor, offering consistent support and stability during uncertain times.

C. Show Empathy

- Acknowledge Feelings: Recognize and validate your partner's emotions and experiences.

- Offer Compassion: Show genuine empathy and understanding, demonstrating that you truly care about their well-being.

D. Be Flexible

- Adapt Together: Be willing to adjust plans and routines as necessary to accommodate new circumstances.

- Compromise: Find common ground and make mutual adjustments to support each other through changes.

E. Problem-Solve Together

- Collaborate: Approach challenges as a team, working together to identify and implement effective solutions.

- Plan Together: Develop and execute strategies to navigate transitions, ensuring both partners are involved in the process.

F. Encourage Self-Care

- Promote Well-being: Suggest and engage in activities that promote relaxation and self-care for both partners.

- Support Health: Encourage and support both physical and emotional self-care practices to maintain overall well-being.

By embracing these strategies, you can provide robust support for each other during times of change, fostering resilience and deepening the strength of your relationship. This proactive and compassionate approach ensures that both partners feel valued, understood, and supported, no matter what changes life brings.

18.4 Celebrating Milestones and Achievements

Celebrating milestones and achievements strengthens your bond and fosters a positive relationship environment. Here's how to celebrate effectively:

A. Acknowledge Milestones

- Recognize Moments: Celebrate important events such as anniversaries, promotions, and personal achievements.

- Importance of Recognition: Highlight the significance of these moments to reinforce the shared journey and accomplishments.

B. Plan Special Celebrations

- Tailored Events: Organize celebrations that specifically reflect the nature of the achievements.

- Personal Touch: Add personalized elements to make the celebrations memorable and meaningful.

C. Give Thoughtful Gifts

- Reflect Interests: Choose gifts that align with and celebrate your partner's specific achievements and interests.

- Show Appreciation: Demonstrate your appreciation and pride with thoughtful and meaningful gifts.

D. Share the Joy

- Celebrate Together: Join in your partner's pride and joy, making their successes a shared experience.

- Enhance Meaning: Amplify the significance of their achievements by celebrating them together.

E. *Reflect on the Journey*

- Discuss Challenges: Talk about the challenges and growth experienced along the journey to the achievement.

- Appreciate Progress: Reflect on the progress made and enhance appreciation for the current accomplishments.

F. *Express Gratitude*

- Show Appreciation: Regularly express gratitude for the shared journey and the progress made together.

- Foster Positivity: Strengthen your bond by reinforcing positive experiences and celebrating shared successes.

By incorporating these practices, you create a supportive and celebratory environment that recognizes and values both individual and shared accomplishments. This approach not only strengthens your bond but also fosters a positive and dynamic relationship.

Chapter 18 Review: Personal Growth and Relationship Development

This chapter outlines strategies for fostering personal growth and relationship development by encouraging each other's dreams, continuing education, supporting each other through changes, and celebrating milestones and achievements.

18.1 Encouraging Each Other's Dreams

- Show Genuine Interest: Actively engage in your partner's aspirations by asking questions and offering support.

- Provide Emotional Support: Be a source of encouragement, offering words of affirmation and motivation during challenging times.

- Celebrate Small Wins: Recognize and celebrate small achievements to reinforce effort and maintain motivation.

- Help Set Goals: Assist in setting realistic, achievable goals and break down larger dreams into manageable steps.

- Offer Practical Help: Provide practical assistance like helping with research or networking.

- Be Patient and Understanding: Acknowledge setbacks and offer a compassionate ear, understanding that the journey has its challenges.

18.2 Continuing Education and Learning Together

- Take Classes Together: Enroll in courses or workshops that interest both of you to learn something new together.

- Read and Discuss Books: Choose books to read together and discuss to stimulate intellectual conversations.

- Attend Seminars and Webinars: Participate in events on topics of mutual interest to stay informed and engaged.

- Explore Online Courses: Use online platforms for flexible learning at your own pace.

- Share Knowledge: Teach each other skills, promoting a culture of continuous learning.

- Set Learning Goals: Establish and pursue learning goals together to stay motivated and achieve new skills.

18.3 Supporting Each Other Through Changes

- Open Communication: Discuss upcoming changes and their potential impacts openly.

- Be a Source of Stability: Provide a reassuring and stable presence during uncertain times.

- Show Empathy: Understand and acknowledge the stress that comes with change, offering compassion.

- Be Flexible: Adapt plans and routines to accommodate new circumstances.

- Problem-Solve Together: Collaborate to find solutions to challenges brought by change.

- Encourage Self-Care: Promote self-care practices to maintain physical and emotional well-being during stressful periods.

18.4 Celebrating Milestones and Achievements

- Acknowledge Milestones: Recognize significant events in both personal and shared lives.

- Plan Special Celebrations: Organize meaningful celebrations tailored to the importance of the milestone.

- Give Thoughtful Gifts: Offer personalized gifts that reflect appreciation and value of the achievements.

- Share the Joy: Celebrate your partner's successes enthusiastically.

- Reflect on the Journey: Discuss the journey and challenges overcome to reach the achievements.

- Express Gratitude: Show appreciation for the shared journey and progress made together.

Summary

Personal growth and relationship development require mutual support, continuous learning, adaptability, and celebration. Encouraging each other's dreams, engaging in ongoing education, supporting each other through changes, and celebrating milestones strengthen your bond and foster a fulfilling partnership. This chapter offers practical steps to grow individually and together, ensuring a successful and enduring relationship.

Part 7: Endings and New Beginnings

Chapter 19: Recognizing When to End a Relationship

Ending a relationship is challenging, but recognizing when it's the right decision is crucial for your well-being and future happiness. This chapter explores how to identify unhealthy patterns, understand when to let go, plan a respectful breakup, and heal and move forward.

19.1 Identifying Unhealthy Patterns

Recognizing unhealthy patterns in a relationship is the first step toward deciding whether it's time to end it. Here are common signs of an unhealthy relationship:

A. Constant Conflict

- Frequent Arguments: Persistent fighting without resolution suggests deeper issues.

- Incompatibility: Ongoing conflict indicates a fundamental mismatch that may be hard to reconcile.

B. Lack of Trust

- Trust Issues: Trust is foundational; its absence is detrimental to the relationship.

- Broken Trust: Repeated breaches of trust undermine the relationship's stability and security.

C. *Emotional or Physical Abuse*

- Abuse Recognition: Any form of emotional or physical abuse is a clear sign to end the relationship immediately.

- Safety Priority: Prioritize your safety and well-being above all else.

D. *Controlling Behavior*

- Autonomy Undermined: Excessive control and dominance negatively affect self-esteem and personal freedom.

- Manipulation: Recognize and address manipulative behaviors that aim to control and undermine.

E. *Persistent Unhappiness*

- Constant Stress: Ongoing unhappiness and stress indicate significant underlying problems.

- Unfulfillment: Chronic dissatisfaction is a red flag that the relationship is not meeting essential emotional needs.

F. *Isolation*

- Social Disconnection: Isolation from friends and family is harmful and often a tactic used by controlling partners.

- External Support: Healthy relationships support and encourage external social connections and independence.

G. Lack of Communication

- Poor Communication: Inadequate communication leads to misunderstandings, resentment, and a breakdown in connection.

- Open Discussion: Open, honest communication is essential for resolving issues and maintaining a strong connection.

Recognizing these unhealthy patterns can help you make informed decisions about the future of your relationship. Prioritizing your well-being and addressing these issues early on can lead to healthier, more fulfilling partnerships.

19.2 Understanding When to Let Go

Knowing when to let go of a relationship is crucial for your emotional health. Here are some indicators that it might be time to move on:

A. Irreconcilable Differences

- Fundamental Differences: Unresolvable differences in values, beliefs, or life goals.

- Incompatibility: Major lifestyle conflicts that cannot be reconciled despite efforts.

B. No Effort to Improve

- Lack of Willingness: One or both partners are unwilling to work on the relationship.

- No Change: Persistent problems remain unresolved due to a lack of effort or commitment.

C. Loss of Respect

- Mutual Respect: Respect is essential for a healthy relationship; its absence is detrimental.

- Irrecoverable Respect: Once respect is lost, it's challenging, if not impossible, to regain.

D. Personal Growth Stagnation

- Hindrance to Growth: The relationship prevents or stifles personal development and growth.

- Goal Achievement: The relationship hinders the achievement of personal goals and aspirations.

E. Emotional Detachment

- Lack of Investment: Emotional withdrawal and lack of interest indicate disengagement.

- Detachment: Persistent emotional detachment is a strong sign of a potential end to the relationship.

F. Constant Negative Impact

- Harmful Effects: The relationship causes more harm than good, affecting overall well-being.

- Mental Health: Persistent negative impact on mental and emotional health suggests it's time to let go.

Recognizing these indicators can help you make a well-informed decision about the future of your relationship. Prioritizing your emotional health and personal growth is essential for leading a fulfilling life.

19.3 Planning a Respectful Breakup

Ending a relationship respectfully minimizes pain and allows both partners to move on healthily. Here's how to plan and execute a respectful breakup:

A. Choose the Right Time and Place

- Private Setting: Select a neutral, private space where you can talk without interruptions.

- Avoid Public Places: Prevent unnecessary embarrassment and ensure privacy.

B. Be Honest but Kind

- Clear Reasons: Explain your reasons for ending the relationship without placing blame.

- Use "I" Statements: Express your feelings and experiences without attacking or blaming your partner.

C. Listen and Acknowledge

- Active Listening: Give your partner the opportunity to express their feelings and thoughts.

- Acknowledge Emotions: Show empathy and understanding of their emotions, validating their experience.

D. Avoid Prolonging the Breakup

- Be Decisive: Clearly communicate your decision to end the relationship.

- No False Hope: Avoid giving mixed signals that might lead to false hope or confusion.

E. Discuss Practical Matters

- Shared Responsibilities: Address practical issues such as living arrangements and shared responsibilities.

- Financial Matters: Discuss and fairly divide any shared financial obligations or assets.

F. Offer Closure

- Address Unresolved Issues: If possible, discuss and resolve any lingering concerns or questions.

- Respectful Goodbye: End the conversation with a respectful and clear goodbye to help both partners move forward.

By following these steps, you can handle the breakup with sensitivity and respect, helping both you and your partner transition to the next phase of your lives with dignity and understanding.

19.4 Healing and Moving Forward

Healing after a breakup is essential for personal growth and preparing for future relationships. Here's how to heal and move forward:

A. Allow Yourself to Grieve

- Acknowledge Feelings: Give yourself time to grieve the loss and accept your emotions.

- Emotional Processing: Understand that feelings of sadness, anger, and confusion are normal parts of the grieving process.

B. Seek Support

- Lean on Friends and Family: Share your feelings with trusted friends and family members who can provide emotional support.

- Professional Help: Consider seeking therapy or counseling for additional guidance and support.

C. Focus on Self-Care

- Physical Well-Being: Engage in healthy activities such as exercise, balanced eating, and sufficient sleep.

- Mental Health: Practice self-care routines, such as meditation, journaling, and taking time for hobbies you enjoy.

D. Reflect and Learn

- Relationship Lessons: Reflect on what you've learned from the relationship and the breakup.

- Future Choices: Use these insights to make more informed decisions in future relationships, recognizing patterns and areas for growth.

E. Set New Goals

- Personal Development: Focus on personal goals and passions that may have been sidelined.

- Redirect Energy: Channel your energy into self-improvement and pursuing new interests and activities.

F. Stay Open to New Beginnings

- Open Mindset: Be open to the possibility of new relationships when you feel ready.

- Wisdom from Experience: Approach new relationships with the wisdom and insights gained from your past experiences.

By following these steps, you can navigate the healing process with grace and prepare yourself for a positive and fulfilling future. Each step helps to rebuild your sense of self, boost your emotional resilience, and pave the way for healthier and more satisfying relationships in the future.

Chapter 19 Review: Recognizing When to End a Relationship

This chapter provides comprehensive guidance on identifying unhealthy relationship patterns, understanding when to let go, planning a respectful breakup, and healing afterward.

19.1 Identifying Unhealthy Patterns

Recognizing unhealthy patterns is the first step in deciding whether to end a relationship. Key signs include:

- Constant Conflict: Frequent, unresolved arguments.

- Lack of Trust: Consistently broken or absent trust.

- Emotional or Physical Abuse: Any form of abuse is a clear danger signal.

- Controlling Behavior: Excessive control or manipulation undermines autonomy.

- Persistent Unhappiness: Ongoing feelings of stress and unfulfillment.

- Isolation: Being cut off from friends, family, or enjoyable activities.

- Lack of Communication: Poor communication leading to misunderstandings and resentment.

19.2 Understanding When to Let Go

Indicators that it might be time to end the relationship include:

- Irreconcilable Differences: Unresolvable differences in values, goals, or lifestyles.

- No Effort to Improve: Unwillingness to work on or change the relationship.

- Loss of Respect: Irrecoverable loss of mutual respect.

- Personal Growth Stagnation: The relationship hinders personal growth.

- Emotional Detachment: Withdrawal from emotional investment in the relationship.

- Constant Negative Impact: Persistent harm to mental, emotional, or physical health.

19.3 Planning a Respectful Breakup

A respectful breakup minimizes pain and allows for healthier moving on:

- Choose the Right Time and Place: Have the conversation in a private, neutral space.

- Be Honest but Kind: Explain your reasons without blaming or attacking.

- Listen and Acknowledge: Let your partner express their feelings and acknowledge them.

- Avoid Prolonging the Breakup: Be decisive and clear to prevent false hope.

- Discuss Practical Matters: Address living arrangements, dividing belongings, and shared responsibilities.

- Offer Closure: Address unresolved issues and say goodbye respectfully.

19.4 Healing and Moving Forward

Steps to heal and move forward after a breakup include:

- Allow Yourself to Grieve: Acknowledge your feelings and give yourself time to grieve.

- Seek Support: Lean on friends, family, or a therapist for support.

- Focus on Self-Care: Engage in activities that promote well-being.

- Reflect and Learn: Understand what went wrong to make better choices in future relationships.

- Set New Goals: Redirect energy towards self-improvement and growth.

- Stay Open to New Beginnings: Approach new relationships with wisdom from past experiences.

Summary

Recognizing when to end a relationship, understanding unhealthy patterns, planning a respectful breakup, and healing afterward are crucial for personal growth and future relationship success. This chapter provides practical steps to navigate the process with dignity, ensuring a healthy transition and new beginnings.

Chapter 20: Rebuilding After a Breakup

Rebuilding your life after a breakup is a journey of self-care, introspection, and growth. This chapter provides comprehensive strategies to heal, learn, and prepare for future possibilities, ensuring you emerge stronger and more resilient.

20.1 Self-Care and Healing

Prioritizing self-care and allowing yourself to heal is essential after a breakup. Here's how to take care of yourself during this time:

A. Allow Yourself to Feel

- Acknowledge Emotions: Accept your feelings, whether it's sadness, anger, or relief.

- Emotional Expression: Don't suppress feelings; express them through journaling, talking, or creative outlets like art or music.

B. Physical Well-Being

- Healthy Lifestyle: Maintain a balanced diet, regular exercise, and adequate sleep to support your physical health.

- Body and Mind Connection: Recognize that taking care of your physical health can boost your emotional well-being.

C. Mental Health Support

- Seek Therapy: Consider professional counseling to help process emotions and gain perspective on your experience.

- Support Networks: Lean on friends and family for emotional support and understanding during this challenging time.

D. Engage in Relaxation Techniques

- Stress Reduction: Practice meditation, yoga, or deep breathing exercises to reduce stress and anxiety.

- Inner Peace: Regular relaxation practices promote calmness and emotional stability.

E. Create a Self-Care Routine

- Personal Enjoyment: Include activities that bring you peace and joy, such as reading, journaling, or nature walks.

- Routine Importance: Establishing a self-care routine helps maintain emotional balance and provides a sense of stability.

F. Avoid Unhealthy Coping Mechanisms

- Healthy Choices: Steer clear of excessive drinking, overeating, or isolating yourself as a means to cope.

- Positive Alternatives: Engage in activities that have a positive impact on your well-being, such as exercise, hobbies, or spending time with loved ones.

By incorporating these self-care practices into your routine, you can navigate the healing process more effectively and rebuild your emotional and physical well-being. Prioritizing self-care helps you move forward with resilience and strength, paving the way for a healthier, happier future.

20.2 Learning from Past Relationships

Reflecting on and learning from your past relationship is crucial for personal growth and future success in relationships. Here's how to gain insights from your experience:

A. Reflect on the Relationship

- Honest Evaluation: Take time to honestly assess what worked well in the relationship and what didn't.

- Role Understanding: Recognize both your role and your partner's role in the relationship dynamics, acknowledging contributions and mistakes.

B. Identify Patterns

- Behavioral Patterns: Look for recurring behaviors or situations that contributed to the breakup.

- Future Choices: Use this awareness to make informed and different choices in future relationships to avoid repeating the same patterns.

C. Recognize Red Flags

- Awareness: Make a list of red flags you may have overlooked or ignored during the relationship.

- Prevention: Learn to recognize these signs earlier in future relationships to prevent similar issues.

D. Acknowledge Positive Aspects

- Growth Recognition: Reflect on the positive experiences and the lessons learned from the relationship.

- Appreciation: Value the personal growth and positive moments that contributed to your development.

E. Take Responsibility

- Accountability: Accept responsibility for your actions and behaviors that may have impacted the relationship.

- Growth Mindset: Use this understanding to foster personal growth and improve future relationships.

F. Set New Relationship Goals

- Clarity: Clearly define what you want and need in a future relationship, setting realistic and healthy expectations.

- Guidance: Let these goals guide you in choosing a compatible partner and building a fulfilling relationship.

By reflecting on your past relationship, identifying patterns, and setting new goals, you can gain valuable insights that will help you grow and prepare for healthier, more successful relationships in the future. This process of self-discovery and learning paves the way for personal development and more fulfilling connections.

20.3 Rebuilding Confidence and Trust

Rebuilding your confidence and trust in yourself and others is vital after a breakup. Here's how to restore these essential aspects:

A. Focus on Self-Improvement

- Personal Goals: Engage in activities that boost self-esteem and confidence, such as pursuing hobbies, setting personal goals, and learning new skills.

- Empowerment: Empower yourself by achieving milestones and celebrating your progress, no matter how small.

B. Positive Self-Talk

- Affirmations: Counter negative thoughts with positive affirmations to reinforce a healthy self-image.

- Self-Compassion: Practice kindness and compassion towards yourself to enhance self-worth and resilience.

C. Set Boundaries

- Healthy Limits: Establish clear boundaries in your interactions to protect your emotional well-being and maintain balance.

- Self-Respect: Boundaries help maintain respect and integrity in relationships, ensuring that your needs are met.

D. Surround Yourself with Positive Influences

- Supportive Network: Spend time with friends and family who uplift and encourage you, providing a positive and nurturing environment.

- Positive Environment: A supportive social circle enhances your confidence and provides a safe space for growth.

E. Gradual Trust-Building

- Small Steps: Start rebuilding trust with small acts and observe the responses, allowing trust to grow gradually.

- Consistent Behavior: Trust is built over time through consistent, reliable actions and transparent communication.

F. Forgive Yourself and Others

- Let Go: Practice forgiveness to let go of past hurts and resentments, freeing yourself from emotional burdens.

- Healing Focus: Focus on healing and moving forward, which aids in restoring trust and preparing for future relationships.

By following these steps, you can rebuild your confidence and trust, laying the foundation for healthier and more fulfilling relationships in the future. This process of self-improvement and positive reinforcement helps you move forward with strength and resilience.

20.4 Opening Yourself to New Possibilities

Opening yourself to new possibilities involves embracing change and being open to new experiences and relationships. Here's how to move forward with an open heart:

A. Embrace Change

- Natural Process: Accept that change is an inherent part of life and personal growth.

- Growth Opportunities: View new beginnings as chances for growth and self-discovery, opening doors to new experiences.

B. Expand Your Social Circle

- New Connections: Join clubs, groups, or activities that interest you to meet new people and expand your social network.

- Diverse Network: Building a diverse network enriches your life and provides varied perspectives and support.

C. Stay Open-Minded

- Avoid Comparisons: Approach new relationships without comparing them to past ones, allowing each connection to develop uniquely.

- Fair Chances: Give new experiences and people a fair chance, embracing the potential for positive outcomes.

D. Set Realistic Expectations

- Patience: Understand that building strong connections takes time, effort, and mutual understanding.

- Healthy Boundaries: Maintain realistic expectations and healthy boundaries in new relationships to foster trust and respect.

E. Explore New Interests

- Personal Fulfillment: Pursue activities and hobbies that excite you and bring joy, enhancing your sense of fulfillment.

- Shared Experiences: Engaging in new interests provides opportunities to meet like-minded individuals and create shared experiences.

F. Be Patient

- Time for Healing: Allow yourself the time to adjust and heal from past experiences, recognizing that healing is a gradual process.

- Future Love: Trust that finding new love and forming meaningful connections will unfold naturally in due time.

Chapter 20 Review: Rebuilding After a Breakup

This chapter offers a comprehensive guide to rebuilding your life after a breakup through self-care, introspection, and growth. It provides strategies for healing, learning from past relationships, rebuilding confidence, and opening yourself to new possibilities.

20.1 Self-Care and Healing

- Allow Yourself to Feel: Acknowledge and accept your emotions to facilitate healing.

- Physical Well-Being: Maintain a healthy lifestyle with nutritious food, regular exercise, and sufficient sleep to support emotional health.

- Mental Health Support: Seek therapy or counseling for professional guidance and support.

- Engage in Relaxation Techniques: Practice meditation, yoga, or deep breathing exercises to reduce stress.

- Create a Self-Care Routine: Include activities you enjoy, such as reading, journaling, or spending time in nature, to promote emotional balance.

- Avoid Unhealthy Coping Mechanisms: Steer clear of excessive drinking, overeating, or isolation to ensure healthy healing.

20.2 Learning from Past Relationships

- Reflect on the Relationship: Identify what worked and what didn't, considering both your and your partner's roles.

- Identify Patterns: Recognize recurring behaviors that contributed to the breakup to avoid repeating them.

- Recognize Red Flags: Note red flags you may have overlooked for better future awareness.

- Acknowledge Positive Aspects: Reflect on the positives and what you learned from them to appreciate your growth.

- Take Responsibility: Accept your actions and behaviors to foster personal growth.

- Set New Relationship Goals: Define what you want in future relationships to guide your choices.

20.3 Rebuilding Confidence and Trust

- Focus on Self-Improvement: Engage in activities that boost self-esteem, such as pursuing hobbies and setting personal goals.

- Positive Self-Talk: Counter negative thoughts with affirmations and self-compassion.

- Set Boundaries: Establish healthy boundaries to protect emotional well-being.

- Surround Yourself with Positive Influences: Spend time with supportive friends and family.

- Gradual Trust-Building: Rebuild trust through small, consistent acts of trustworthiness.

- Forgive Yourself and Others: Let go of past hurts to move forward and rebuild trust.

20.4 Opening Yourself to New Possibilities

- Embrace Change: Accept and embrace new beginnings as opportunities for growth.

- Expand Your Social Circle: Meet new people through clubs, groups, or activities.

- Stay Open-Minded: Approach new relationships with an open heart, avoiding comparisons to the past.

- Set Realistic Expectations: Understand that building strong connections takes time and effort.

- Explore New Interests: Pursue activities that excite you to enrich your life and meet like-minded individuals.

- Be Patient: Give yourself time to heal and adjust, understanding that finding new love is a gradual process.

Summary

Rebuilding after a breakup involves self-care, learning, confidence-building, and opening yourself to new possibilities. By focusing on these areas, you can move forward with strength and optimism, ensuring personal growth and readiness for future relationships. This chapter provides practical guidance to help you navigate this transformative period, fostering a positive outlook and a brighter future.

Chapter 21: New Beginnings

Embarking on new beginnings after the end of a relationship involves embracing change, rediscovering yourself, envisioning a bright future, and opening your heart to new love. This chapter provides comprehensive strategies to navigate this transformative journey effectively.

21.1 Embracing Change and Growth

Embracing change is essential for personal growth and moving forward. Here's how to welcome change and foster growth:

A. Accept the Past

- Acknowledge What Happened: Recognize the end of your relationship as an integral part of your life journey.

- Opportunity for Growth: Understand that each ending brings new beginnings and opportunities for personal development.

B. Adopt a Growth Mindset

- View Challenges as Opportunities: Focus on learning and improving through each experience, viewing challenges as opportunities for growth.

- Stepping Stones: Embrace setbacks as essential steps toward greater achievements and personal fulfillment.

C. Set New Goals

- Define Personal and Professional Goals: Establish new goals that excite and motivate you, both personally and professionally.

- Vision Board: Create a vision board to visualize and manifest your aspirations, keeping your goals in focus.

D. Stay Positive

- Maintain a Positive Outlook: Surround yourself with positivity and avoid dwelling on negative thoughts or experiences.

- Practice Gratitude: Regularly reflect on what you are thankful for to enhance your positivity and overall well-being.

E. Seek Inspiration

- Learn from Others: Find inspiration from books, podcasts, mentors, or individuals who have navigated similar transitions successfully.

- Join Communities: Engage with communities or groups that inspire and motivate you, providing support and encouragement.

F. Celebrate Progress

- Recognize Achievements: Acknowledge and celebrate your progress, no matter how small, to maintain motivation and enthusiasm.

- Reward Yourself: Reward yourself for milestones achieved to reinforce your commitment to growth and personal development.

By embracing change and focusing on growth, you can move forward with confidence and resilience, opening yourself up to new opportunities and a fulfilling future.

21.2 Rediscovering Yourself

Rediscovering yourself is crucial for personal fulfillment and readiness for new relationships. Here's how to reconnect with your true self:

A. Reflect on Your Interests

- Reconnect with Hobbies: Reflect on hobbies or activities you love and that bring you joy, reigniting old passions.

- Explore New Activities: Consider new activities that intrigue you and that you've always wanted to try, expanding your horizons.

B. Practice Self-Compassion

- Be Kind to Yourself: Acknowledge your strengths and forgive yourself for past mistakes, fostering a healthy self-image.

- Treat Yourself Well: Treat yourself with the same understanding and care you would offer a friend, nurturing your emotional well-being.

C. Prioritize Self-Care

- Engage in Nourishing Activities: Participate in activities that nourish your mind, body, and soul, promoting holistic health.

- Establish a Routine: Create a daily self-care routine that includes time for relaxation and activities that bring you happiness and peace.

D. Build Self-Confidence

- Focus on Achievements: Build your self-confidence through recognizing personal achievements and using positive affirmations.

- Celebrate Successes: Celebrate your successes, both big and small, and remind yourself of your worth and capabilities.

E. Reconnect with Values

- Evaluate Core Values: Reevaluate your core values and ensure your actions align with them, providing clarity and direction.

- Live Authentically: Make choices that reflect what matters most to you, bringing inner peace and satisfaction through authentic living.

By focusing on these aspects, you can rediscover your true self, fostering personal growth and preparing yourself for healthier, more fulfilling relationships in the future.

21.3 Building a New Vision for the Future

Creating a fresh outlook on life after a significant change is an empowering step towards new beginnings. Here's how to effectively build a new vision for the future in the context of dating and relationships:

A. Clarify Your Aspirations

1. Define Your Relationship Goals:

- Specificity: Clearly define what you want to achieve in your personal relationships, such as finding a compatible partner, building a supportive social circle, or improving your existing relationship.

- Long-Term Vision: Establish both short-term and long-term relationship goals. Consider where you want to be in one, five, or ten years in terms of your romantic and social connections.

2. Visualize Success:

- Mental Imagery: Spend time visualizing your ideal relationship and the steps needed to achieve it. Imagine the qualities you want in a partner, the activities you'd enjoy together, and the feelings you wish to cultivate.

- Vision Board: Create a vision board with images and words that represent your ideal relationship. Place it somewhere you will see daily to keep you inspired and focused.

B. Develop a Strategic Plan

1. Action Steps:

- Break It Down: Divide your relationship goals into actionable steps. Identify what needs to be done daily, weekly, and monthly to move closer to your vision.

- Prioritize Tasks: Focus on activities that will significantly advance your relationship goals, such as attending social events, joining dating platforms, or improving communication skills.

2. Seek Guidance:

- Mentorship: Find mentors or coaches who can provide advice, support, and accountability in your dating and relationship journey. Their experience can offer valuable insights and help you navigate challenges.

- Continuous Learning: Engage in continuous learning through books, workshops, and online courses on relationships. Staying informed can provide new perspectives and skills necessary for building healthy connections.

C. Cultivate a Positive Mindset

1. Embrace Positivity:

- Affirmations: Use positive affirmations to reinforce a positive mindset about dating and relationships. Statements like "I am worthy of love" or "I attract healthy and fulfilling relationships" can boost your confidence.

- Gratitude Practice: Regularly practice gratitude by reflecting on what you are thankful for in your relationships and personal life. This can help maintain a positive outlook and attract more positive experiences.

2. Overcome Obstacles:

- Resilience: Develop resilience by viewing dating challenges as opportunities for growth. Learn from past relationship experiences and use them to strengthen your resolve.

- Support System: Surround yourself with supportive and positive individuals who encourage and uplift you. A strong support system can provide the emotional strength needed to persevere in your dating journey.

D. Stay Flexible and Adaptable

1. Adjust as Needed:

- Flexibility: Be willing to adapt your relationship plans as circumstances change. Flexibility allows you to navigate unexpected challenges without losing sight of your goals.

- Open-Mindedness: Stay open to new opportunities and perspectives in dating. Sometimes, unexpected paths can lead to even greater relationships.

2. Regular Review:

- Progress Tracking: Regularly review your progress towards your relationship goals. Reflect on what is working well and what needs adjustment.

- Celebrate Milestones: Acknowledge and celebrate your relationship achievements along the way. Recognizing your progress boosts motivation and keeps you engaged.

By clarifying your relationship aspirations, developing a strategic plan, cultivating a positive mindset, and staying flexible, you can build a new vision for your future that is both inspiring and achievable. This fresh outlook will not only guide you towards healthier and more fulfilling relationships but also enhance your overall sense of purpose and happiness.

21.4 Finding Love Again

Finding love again is a beautiful part of new beginnings. Here's how to approach new relationships with an open heart:

A. Heal Fully First

- Take Time to Heal: Ensure you have taken the necessary time to process your past relationship and its ending.

- Clear Heart and Mind: Enter a new relationship with emotional clarity and readiness, free from past baggage.

B. Know What You Want

- Reflect on Lessons Learned: Identify what you want and need in a new partner based on past experiences.

- List Qualities and Values: Make a list of qualities and values that are important to you in a partner, ensuring alignment with your core values.

C. Be Open-Minded

- Avoid Comparisons: Approach new relationships without comparing them to past ones, allowing each connection to be unique.

- Give Fair Chances: Embrace each new connection as a unique opportunity, open to what it may bring.

D. Take Things Slow

- Allow Natural Development: Let new relationships develop at their own pace, without rushing.

- Build a Solid Foundation: Take the time to get to know your new partner and establish a strong, stable connection.

E. Communicate Clearly

- Practice Open Communication: Establish clear, honest communication from the beginning of the relationship.

- Discuss Expectations and Boundaries: Talk openly about your expectations, boundaries, and feelings to ensure mutual understanding.

F. Trust Your Instincts

- Listen to Your Inner Voice: Trust your gut feelings and intuition regarding new relationships.

- Respect Your Instincts: Follow your instincts when something feels right or wrong, honoring your inner voice.

G. Enjoy the Journey

- Focus on Connection: Enjoy getting to know new people and building meaningful connections.

- Embrace Possibilities: Appreciate the excitement and potential of new beginnings, savoring each moment.

By following these guidelines, you can approach new relationships with confidence and an open heart, ready to embrace the joy and potential of finding love again.

Chapter 21 Review: New Beginnings

This chapter offers comprehensive strategies to help you navigate new beginnings after the end of a relationship by embracing change, rediscovering yourself, envisioning a bright future, and opening your heart to new love.

21.1 Embracing Change and Growth

- Accept the Past: Acknowledge the end of the relationship and see it as part of your journey.

- Adopt a Growth Mindset: View challenges as opportunities for self-improvement.

- Set New Goals: Define personal and professional goals that inspire you.

- Stay Positive: Maintain a positive outlook and surround yourself with positivity.

- Seek Inspiration: Find motivation from books, podcasts, mentors, or people who have navigated similar transitions.

- Celebrate Progress: Recognize and celebrate even small achievements to reinforce your resilience.

21.2 Rediscovering Yourself

- Reflect on Your Interests: Reconnect with hobbies and activities that bring you joy.

- Explore New Opportunities: Try new experiences to discover new passions and strengths.

- Practice Self-Compassion: Be kind to yourself, acknowledge your strengths, and forgive past mistakes.

- Prioritize Self-Care: Engage in activities that nourish your mind, body, and soul.

- Build Self-Confidence: Focus on personal achievements and positive affirmations to enhance self-esteem.

- Reconnect with Values: Reevaluate your core values and align your actions with them for authentic living.

21.3 Building a New Vision for the Future

- Visualize Your Ideal Life: Spend time envisioning your ideal future across various aspects of life.

- Set Clear Goals: Break down your vision into achievable goals using the SMART criteria.

- Create a Plan: Develop a step-by-step plan to reach your goals and outline necessary actions and resources.

- Stay Flexible: Be adaptable and willing to adjust your plans as needed.

- Seek Support: Surround yourself with supportive people who believe in your vision.

- Monitor Progress: Regularly review your progress, celebrate achievements, and adjust plans as necessary.

21.4 Finding Love Again

- Heal Fully First: Take time to heal and process your past relationship before entering a new one.

- Know What You Want: Reflect on past relationships to identify what you want in a new partner.

- Be Open-Minded: Approach new relationships with an open mind and avoid comparisons to past partners.

- Take Things Slow: Allow new relationships to develop naturally without rushing.

- Communicate Clearly: Practice open and honest communication from the start.

- Trust Your Instincts: Listen to your intuition and trust your gut feelings about new relationships.

- Enjoy the Journey: Focus on enjoying the process of getting to know new people and building connections.

Summary

New beginnings after a relationship end offer opportunities for transformation and personal growth. By embracing change, rediscovering yourself, building a new vision for the future, and opening yourself to new love, you can create a fulfilling and joyful life. This chapter provides practical, step-by-step guidance to help you navigate this exciting phase with confidence and optimism, ensuring a successful transition to a bright and promising future.

Conclusion

Reflecting on Your Relationship Journey

Reflecting on your relationship journey is essential for understanding your growth and experiences. It allows you to appreciate the lessons learned and the progress made. Here's how to reflect effectively:

1. Review Milestones and Achievements

- Celebrate Progress: Look back at significant milestones and achievements in your relationships. Reflect on anniversaries, shared accomplishments, and personal triumphs.

- Overcome Challenges: Celebrate the progress you've made and the challenges you've overcome together.

2. Identify Key Learnings

- Communication Insights: Reflect on the key lessons you've learned about communication, compromise, and emotional intelligence.

- Relationship Growth: Consider how these insights have shaped your understanding of love and partnership.

3. Acknowledge Growth

- Personal Development: Recognize the personal growth you've experienced through your relationships.

- Strength and Wisdom: Acknowledge how you've become stronger, wiser, and more self-aware.

4. Appreciate the Journey

- Embrace Experiences: Appreciate the journey itself, including the ups and downs. Each experience has contributed to your understanding and ability to build healthier relationships.

- Full Spectrum of Emotions: Embrace the full spectrum of emotions and experiences as integral parts of your growth.

5. Journal Your Thoughts

- Writing for Clarity: Consider journaling your reflections. Writing down your thoughts can provide clarity and a deeper understanding of your relationship journey.

- Track Progress: Regular journaling helps track your progress and offers a space for introspection.

6. Discuss with Your Partner

- Share Insights: If you're in a relationship, discuss your reflections with your partner. Sharing your insights can strengthen your bond and mutual understanding.

- Open Dialogue: Open dialogues about past experiences and future goals can enhance your relationship.

By reflecting on your relationship journey, you gain valuable insights that help you appreciate your growth, understand past experiences, and prepare for a healthier and more fulfilling future.

Continuing to Grow and Learn

Personal growth and continuous learning are vital for maintaining a fulfilling relationship. Here's how to ensure ongoing growth:

1. Set Personal and Relationship Goals

- Self-Improvement: Continuously set new personal and relationship goals to aim for self-improvement and enhancing your partnership.

- Direction and Motivation: Goals provide direction and motivation for continuous development.

2. Embrace Lifelong Learning

- Expand Knowledge: Adopt a mindset of lifelong learning by seeking to expand your knowledge and skills through books, courses, and workshops.

- Stay Curious: Remain open to new ideas and perspectives to keep your mind engaged and adaptable.

3. Stay Open to Feedback

- Constructive Criticism: Be open to feedback from your partner and others, embracing it as a tool for improvement.

- Opportunities for Growth: View feedback as an opportunity for growth rather than criticism, using it to refine and enhance your approach.

4. Practice Self-Reflection

- Regular Assessments: Regularly practice self-reflection to stay aware of your thoughts, feelings, and behaviors.

- Awareness and Development: This awareness is crucial for personal development and helps in making informed decisions.

5. Cultivate Resilience

- Emotional Strength: Develop resilience to handle life's challenges, strengthening your emotional resilience to navigate difficulties.

- Positive Outlook: Resilience enables you to bounce back from setbacks and grow stronger, maintaining a positive outlook.

6. Maintain Healthy Relationships

- Supportive Network: Surround yourself with supportive and positive relationships, as healthy connections with friends and family provide a strong foundation for personal and relational growth.

- Sense of Belonging: A supportive network fosters a sense of belonging and security, essential for overall well-being.

7. Engage in New Experiences

- Stepping Out: Embrace new experiences and challenges, stepping out of your comfort zone for significant personal growth.

- Shared Activities: Trying new activities together can reignite passion and interest, enhancing your connection.

Final Thoughts

Building and maintaining healthy relationships is an ongoing journey that requires effort, understanding, and a commitment to growth. By reflecting on your past experiences and continuously striving to learn and improve, you can cultivate fulfilling and meaningful relationships.

This guide has provided you with practical tools, insights, and strategies to navigate the complexities of dating and relationships. From understanding yourself and effective communication to managing conflicts and embracing new beginnings, each chapter offers valuable guidance to help you build a strong, loving, and enduring partnership.

As you move forward, remember that every relationship is unique, and there is no one-size-fits-all approach. Be patient with yourself and your partner, stay open to learning, and cherish the journey of growing together. With dedication and a positive mindset, you can create and sustain a relationship that brings joy, love, and fulfillment into your life.

Final Note

Thank you for reading the HowExpert Guide to Dating and Relationships. We hope this book has provided you with the tools and inspiration to create the loving and lasting relationship you deserve. Remember, the journey of love is a continuous process of learning, growing, and connecting. Enjoy every moment of it.

Appendices

Glossary of Dating & Relationship Terms from A to Z

Understanding key terms can help you navigate the complexities of dating and relationships. Here's a comprehensive glossary of common relationship terms from A to Z:

- Affection: Physical or emotional expressions of love and care, such as hugging, kissing, or kind words, that strengthen bonds between partners.

- Attachment Style: A psychological model describing how individuals form emotional bonds and relationships, often based on early childhood experiences. Common styles include secure, anxious, avoidant, and disorganized. Understanding your attachment style can help improve relationship dynamics and personal growth.

- Boundaries: Personal limits set in relationships to ensure respect, safety, and well-being. These can be physical, emotional, or digital. Establishing healthy boundaries is crucial for maintaining individuality and mutual respect in relationships.

- Codependency: A relationship dynamic where one partner is overly reliant on the other for emotional support and self-esteem, often leading to unhealthy patterns. Recognizing and addressing codependency can lead to healthier, more balanced relationships.

- Compatibility: The degree to which partners are well-matched in terms of values, interests, and goals. High compatibility often leads to more harmonious relationships.

- Conflict Resolution: Strategies and processes used to resolve disagreements and conflicts in a healthy and constructive manner. Effective conflict resolution skills are essential for maintaining harmony and understanding in relationships.

- Deal Breakers: Specific traits or behaviors that are unacceptable to an individual in a relationship, often leading to a decision to end the relationship.

- Emotional Intelligence: The ability to understand, manage, and express emotions effectively, both personally and in relationships. High emotional intelligence contributes to better communication, empathy, and conflict resolution.

- Empathy: The ability to understand and share the feelings of another person, which is crucial for building emotional connections and understanding in relationships.

- Forgiveness: The process of letting go of resentment and anger towards someone who has wronged you, essential for healing and maintaining healthy relationships.

- Gaslighting: A form of manipulation where one person makes the other doubt their own reality, perception, or memories. Recognizing gaslighting is critical for protecting one's mental health and autonomy.

- Honeymoon Phase: The early stage of a relationship characterized by intense emotions, excitement, and infatuation. This phase is often marked by idealization and a strong desire to spend time together.

- Intimacy: A close, familiar, and usually affectionate or loving personal relationship with another person. Intimacy can be emotional, physical, or intellectual.

- Jealousy: An emotion that arises when a person feels threatened by a third party who is perceived to be a rival for their partner's affections. Managing jealousy is important for maintaining trust and security in relationships.

- Kindness: The quality of being friendly, generous, and considerate. Kindness is essential for fostering a loving and supportive relationship.

- Love Languages: A concept introduced by Dr. Gary Chapman, identifying five primary ways people express and receive love: words of affirmation, acts of service, receiving gifts, quality time, and physical touch. Understanding love languages can enhance emotional connections and relationship satisfaction.

- Monogamy: A relationship structure where an individual has only one partner at a time, which is often contrasted with polyamory or open relationships.

- Nonverbal Communication: The process of conveying information without words, including body language, facial expressions, and tone of voice. Nonverbal cues play a significant role in expressing emotions and intentions.

- Open Relationship: A consensual relationship structure where partners agree that they may engage in romantic or sexual relationships with other people.

- Polyamory: A relationship structure where individuals have consensual romantic or sexual relationships with multiple partners simultaneously. It emphasizes openness, honesty, and mutual consent.

- Quality Time: One of the five love languages, referring to giving undivided attention to a partner to strengthen the relationship.

- Red Flags: Warning signs or behaviors that indicate potential problems or unhealthy dynamics in a relationship. Identifying red flags early can prevent future emotional distress and unhealthy patterns.

- Respect: A fundamental element in relationships, involving recognizing and valuing each other's boundaries, feelings, and autonomy.

- Self-Love: The practice of taking care of oneself and maintaining self-respect and self-worth. Self-love is crucial for healthy relationships as it forms the basis of how individuals treat others.

- Trust: The firm belief in the reliability, truth, ability, or strength of someone, essential for healthy relationships. Building and maintaining trust is foundational for long-term relationship success.

- Understanding: The ability to comprehend the feelings, thoughts, and behaviors of a partner, which is crucial for empathy and effective communication in relationships.

- Vulnerability: The willingness to open up and share personal thoughts, feelings, and experiences with a partner. Vulnerability fosters deeper connections and emotional intimacy.

- Withdrawal: The act of pulling away emotionally or physically from a partner, often as a response to conflict or stress. Recognizing and addressing withdrawal behaviors can help maintain connection and resolve issues.

- X-Factor: The unique qualities or traits that make someone particularly attractive or interesting to their partner, contributing to the special dynamics of the relationship.

- Yearning: A deep, emotional longing for someone, often experienced in the context of romantic relationships. Yearning can drive emotional closeness and desire.

- Zest: Enthusiasm and energy in a relationship, often reflected in the excitement and passion partners feel towards each other. Maintaining zest can keep the relationship vibrant and engaging.

By familiarizing yourself with these terms, you can enhance your understanding of relationship dynamics and improve your ability to navigate and nurture your relationships.

Recommended Reading and Resources

Enhance your understanding of relationships with these carefully curated books, websites, podcasts, worksheets, and other resources. Each recommendation is designed to provide valuable insights and practical advice for building and maintaining healthy, fulfilling relationships.

Books

- "The 5 Love Languages" by Gary Chapman: This classic guide helps you discover the five primary ways people express and receive love, enhancing your ability to connect deeply with your partner.

- "Attached: The New Science of Adult Attachment and How It Can Help You Find—and Keep—Love" by Amir Levine and Rachel Heller: Learn about different attachment styles and how they influence your relationships, helping you foster stronger, more secure bonds.

- "Hold Me Tight: Seven Conversations for a Lifetime of Love" by Dr. Sue Johnson: Explore Emotionally Focused Therapy principles to strengthen your emotional connection and resolve conflicts more effectively.

- "The Seven Principles for Making Marriage Work" by John Gottman and Nan Silver: Discover research-backed strategies for maintaining a healthy, long-lasting marriage from one of the foremost experts in relationship science.

- "Men Are from Mars, Women Are from Venus" by John Gray: Understand and appreciate the fundamental differences between men and women to improve communication and deepen your connection.

- "Daring Greatly" by Brené Brown: Embrace vulnerability and authenticity as keys to creating deeper, more meaningful relationships.

Websites and Online Resources

- Psychology Today: www.psychologytoday.com

  A comprehensive resource offering articles and expert advice on relationships, mental health, and personal development.

- The Gottman Institute: www.gottman.com

  Access research-based tools and resources for building strong, healthy relationships from the leaders in relationship science.

- Love is Respect: www.loveisrespect.org

  Find resources and support for fostering healthy relationships and preventing abuse, including information on setting boundaries and recognizing warning signs.

- Relate: www.relate.org.uk

  Get professional relationship support and counseling services, along with helpful articles and advice on various relationship issues.

Podcasts

- "Where Should We Begin?" with Esther Perel: Gain insights into relationship dynamics through real-life couples therapy sessions conducted by renowned psychotherapist Esther Perel.

- "The Love, Happiness and Success Podcast" with Dr. Lisa Marie Bobby: Receive expert advice on relationships, personal growth, and achieving happiness from a licensed marriage and family therapist.

- "The Gottman Institute Podcast": Learn practical tips and strategies for building strong, healthy relationships based on the renowned Gottman Method.

Worksheets and Exercises

Practical worksheets and exercises can help you apply the concepts learned in this guide. Here are some useful tools:

- Relationship Check-In Worksheet: A tool for regularly assessing the health of your relationship and addressing any concerns. This worksheet helps partners stay aligned and connected by encouraging open dialogue about their relationship.

- Communication Skills Exercise: Activities designed to enhance your communication abilities, including active listening and expressing feelings. These exercises foster better understanding and empathy between partners.

- Conflict Resolution Plan: A step-by-step guide for resolving conflicts constructively. This plan provides a structured approach to addressing disagreements and finding mutually satisfying solutions.

- Love Languages Quiz: A quiz to help you and your partner identify your primary love languages and learn how to express love effectively. Understanding each other's love languages can deepen emotional bonds and relationship satisfaction.

- Goal Setting Worksheet: A template for setting and tracking personal and relationship goals. This worksheet helps couples set clear, achievable goals and create a shared vision for their future.

Contact Information for Relationship Support Services

If you need additional support, consider reaching out to these professional services:

- _Therapists and Counselors:_

- Psychology Today Therapist Directory: www.psychologytoday.com/us/therapists - Find a therapist near you.

- BetterHelp: www.betterhelp.com - Online counseling and therapy services.

- Talkspace: www.talkspace.com - Online therapy with licensed professionals.

- _Relationship Coaching:_

- Tony Robbins Relationship Coaching: www.tonyrobbins.com/coaching/relationship-coaching/ - Professional coaching to help improve your relationship dynamics and achieve greater connection.

- Relationship Hero: www.relationshiphero.com - Professional relationship coaching services.

- _Crisis Support:_

- National Domestic Violence Hotline: 1-800-799-SAFE (7233) or www.thehotline.org

- Crisis Text Line: Text HOME to 741741 for 24/7 support.

About the Publisher HowExpert

HowExpert publishes quick 'how to' guides on all topics from A to Z. Visit www.howexpert.com for more information on our wide range of titles and to find more books on relationships and personal development. We strive to provide practical, concise, and insightful guides that empower readers to tackle new challenges and learn new skills.

Thank you for choosing the HowExpert Guide to Dating and Relationships. We hope this book has provided you with the tools, knowledge, and inspiration to create and maintain a loving and enduring relationship. Remember, the journey of love is an ongoing process of learning, growing, and connecting. Enjoy every step of it!

About the Author

HowExpert publishes how to guides on all topics from A to Z. Visit HowExpert.com to learn more.

About the Publisher

Byungjoon "BJ" Min is an author, publisher, entrepreneur, and the founder of HowExpert. He started off as a once broke convenience store clerk to eventually becoming a fulltime internet marketer and finding his niche in publishing. He is the founder and publisher of HowExpert where the mission is to discover, empower, and maximize everyday people's talents to ultimately make a positive impact in the world for all topics from A to Z. Visit BJMin.com and HowExpert.com to learn more. John 14:6

Recommended Resources

- HowExpert.com – How To Guides on All Topics from A to Z by Everyday Experts.
- HowExpert.com/free – Free HowExpert Email Newsletter.
- HowExpert.com/books – HowExpert Books
- HowExpert.com/courses – HowExpert Courses
- HowExpert.com/clothing – HowExpert Clothing
- HowExpert.com/membership – HowExpert Membership Site
- HowExpert.com/affiliates – HowExpert Affiliate Program
- HowExpert.com/jobs – HowExpert Jobs
- HowExpert.com/writers – Write About Your #1 Passion/Knowledge/Expertise & Become a HowExpert Author.
- HowExpert.com/resources – Additional HowExpert Recommended Resources
- YouTube.com/HowExpert – Subscribe to HowExpert YouTube.
- Instagram.com/HowExpert – Follow HowExpert on Instagram.
- Facebook.com/HowExpert – Follow HowExpert on Facebook.
- TikTok.com/@HowExpert – Follow HowExpert on TikTok.

www.ingramcontent.com/pod-product-compliance
Ingram Content Group UK Ltd.
Pitfield, Milton Keynes, MK11 3LW, UK
UKHW040839310325
5234UKWH00002B/29